ON THE BLUNT EDGE

ON THE BLUNT EDGE

Technology in Composition's History and Pedagogy

Edited by Shane Borrowman

Parlor Press
Anderson, South Carolina
www.parlorpress.com

Parlor Press LLC, Anderson, South Carolina, USA

© 2012 by Parlor Press
All rights reserved.
Printed in the United States of America

SAN: 254-8879

Library of Congress Cataloging-in-Publication Data

On the blunt edge : technology in composition's history and pedagogy /
edited by Shane Borrowman.
    p. cm.
Includes bibliographical references and index.
ISBN 978-1-60235-220-9 (pbk. : alk. paper) -- ISBN 978-1-60235-221-6
(alk. paper) -- ISBN 978-1-60235-222-3 (adobe ebook) -- ISBN 978-1-
60235-223-0 (epub)
1. English language--Rhetoric--Study and teaching (Higher) 2. English
philology--Study and teaching--History. I. Borrowman, Shane.
PE1404.O487 2011
421'.1028--dc22

                        2011011270

Cover design by David Blakesley.
Printed on acid-free paper.

Parlor Press, LLC is an independent publisher of scholarly and trade titles
in print and multimedia formats. This book is available in paper, cloth and
Adobe eBook formats from Parlor Press on the World Wide Web at http://
www.parlorpress.com or through online and brick-and-mortar bookstores.
For submission information or to find out about Parlor Press publications,
write to Parlor Press, 3015 Brackenberry Drive, Anderson, South Carolina,
29621, or email editor@parlorpress.com.

Contents

Introduction: Process and Place, Technology in a Glass

Shane Borrowman

> *Although possibly now threatened by discs as a medium for recording the printed word, the book is still regarded by many as an ideal information recording and transfer medium (28).*

> —Charles T. Meadow, *Ink into Bits*

The story of my writing process is a story of place: I remember *what* I wrote through remembering *where* I wrote. My first published poem was written in Morrison #307, the dorm room at Eastern Washington University where I lived for three years. The TV was playing Sunday night news programs, and the smell of urine was strong. When my roommate was too drunk to stagger to the bathroom, he peed in our garbage can. This happened so often that the bottom of the can rusted out, quickly developing both a stink and scabrous, crusty edged holes. My first article on pedagogy—penned for a regional *English Journal* affiliate—was written in the sunbeam that came into my breakfast nook from six to seven o'clock during June and July mornings. The apartment was half of the top floor of a former boardinghouse, and the galley kitchen had so little counter space that my microwave sat atop the refrigerator. My last poem was written while parked on I-90, near Missoula, Montana, waiting for the tow truck to come and rocking with the windblast from passing semitrucks. The most recent article on pedagogy was written in my office at Gonzaga University, with the bells from St. Al's cathedral tolling just outside the window. I wrote a lot in that office, including the proposals for both my first edited collection and first textbook, and there were always bells. St. Al's was the neighborhood place of worship, and not a week went by when there wasn't a marrying or burying. The burials came with bagpipes to supplement the bells.

The list could continue virtually *ad nauseum,* could include more poetry, more articles, two theses and a dissertation, other collections and textbooks and proposals. I wrote in rental duplexes while neighbors argued loudly next door, sometimes slamming one another against our shared wall. I wrote while floating on a raft in the Tucson sun. I wrote in cars that reeked from my cigarettes and in cars I bought after I quit smoking. The list could continue, but it would never get any closer to being accurate. The story of my writing process, I have always mistakenly thought, is a story of place. Location anchors the narrative scraps of memory nicely, but memory is a variable that, I have come to realize, doesn't matter much for me. Wherever I happen to be writing, I am still the writer. The poet sitting in Morrison #307 smelling rust and urine is the researcher sitting in his Troll's Den at the University of Nevada, Reno—departmental slang for the office that's beneath a footbridge. Places change, but places don't change the writer.

Rather than focusing on place, my thoughts on my writing process focus more and more on the story of technology, on the changes reflected in/wrought by technologies of writing. My first poem was written longhand, in blue Bic ink, in a flat-bound notebook. The cover of this notebook was bent and torn and marked with coffee rings; it was where my creative writing happened, including "Cold Warrior"—two or three stanzas of free verse written during a *60 Minutes* biography of then Secretary of Defense Dick Cheney. That poem happened because of pen, paper, and TV, and its publication marked the beginning of my professional life, although I wouldn't realize this for nearly twenty years. For half that time, I continued to write poetry. Always longhand in blue ink. Always in those same flat-bound notebooks filled with non college-ruled paper.

My nonfiction writing never happened longhand after seventh or eighth grade. In high school I drafted on a Commodore 64, saving on 5 ¼" floppy disks and printing dot matrix. A typewriter with correction tape carried me through the first years of college, while a Brother word processor—fold-down keyboard hiding a monochromatic orange/black screen—that weighed in at maybe thirty pounds sufficed until I began my thesis on Norman Maclean. The Macintosh Quadra 650 that drafted that thesis served me well for four years, through a second MA program and into my PhD. And so on. Somewhere along the narrative arc, I switched to a Toshiba laptop that weighed just under fifteen pounds—a laptop I hated almost from the beginning and that I gave to Goodwill after it sat unused in a closet for several years. Two or three Dell desktop computers came and went, plus school-owned systems, including the one on which I write these words. If I were working at home, then I would be using my laptop, since my desktop system has been relegated to a dusty table in the garage, where it sits almost unused.

I no longer write poetry—no longer write much of anything longhand, other than notes-to-self and marginal/terminal comments on my students' essays. My cycle of purchasing and discarding computers seems to be accelerating, at least in part because of dropping prices and rising financial resources.

On the Blunt Edge began as a proposal typed in Reno. While that proposal made its way through the physical labyrinth of the postal system, all communication that followed has been via email, including my correspondence with contributors, some of whom I have never met face-to-face. Might *never* meet face-to-face. Although the manuscript has come together through the interaction of Dell hardware and Microsoft software—and thousands of miles of cable—the idea for this book had its genesis in a strangely technology-rich experience.

I sat atop a bar stool in the Seattle-Tacoma Airport, drinking a beer brewed locally and waiting for my connecting flight to Atlanta. I was typing on a full-size foldout keyboard attached to my Palm Pilot and trolling through my much-annotated copy of George Kennedy's translation of Aristotle's *Rhetoric*. My cellular phone sat, open, beside my beer, and I was using it to check my email on America Online. Beneath the phone sat my tiny composition book with its marble-patterned cover. The television hanging above the bar broadcast live CNN coverage from the Afghan theatre of operations in the ongoing war on terror, the footage itself comprised mostly of black-and-white video from an unmanned drone—a weapon's eye view of an attack carried out only hours before in mountains literally half a planet away.

The moment was ripe for reflection: travel across nearly the breadth of the nation to speak at a conference, travel via the technology of flight, itself less than a century old; notes taken on inexpensive paper in a notebook bound in China; notes in the margins of a book so easy to replace that I don't hesitate to defile it as needed; typing on a keyboard small enough to fold into my suit coat pocket, a keyboard attached to a computer small enough to fit in the other pocket; a telephone that worked virtually anywhere in the country and didn't require me to pack a roll of quarters, allowing me access to private email on a service that wasn't even connected to the Web when I first signed on in the early 1990s, when online time still went for a market price of five hours per month for twenty dollars; pictures from a war zone recorded not by a correspondent or warrior but by the weapon itself and presented visually on a technology present in most American homes for less than half a century.

The moment was overwhelming, and I suddenly felt clueless. I was typing—a skill learned in high school on a battered electric IBM—because I was incapable of writing longhand for any length of time without suffering hand and wrist pain. I was reading the most recent translation of the *Rhetoric*, but I had, quite literally, no idea how the text of that work had survived for more than two millennia. I had only the vaguest notions about how an airplane worked. I knew nothing about cellular technology and only slightly more about television. Running my eyes over the miscellany before me, I realized the only thing I understood in this entire situation was in my glass.

I knew how to brew beer and could, if called upon, either describe how to make the beverage before me or, with minimal time and tools, produce a reasonable duplicate. Everything else was either little-understood or completely unknown, from paper to pen to the physical printing and binding of books. Even the process that produced the glass itself was mysterious. Heated sand might be involved. Is a beer schooner blown? Poured in some kind of mold?

On the Blunt Edge began on that bar stool, began not as I looked for answers to all of those techno-mysteries before me but as I realized that I had, quite literally, no idea how to go about finding answers . . . or even formulating answerable questions. My ignorance was broad and deep, and its connections to my profession in rhetoric and composition seemed like a cause for concern. I could live with my ignorance of glassware and cellular telephones and fixed-wing flight; as a teacher of writing and a teacher of teachers of writing, my ignorance of the various media of communication was more damning and damaging. I was as ignorant of the process of paper-making as I was of the art of telegraphy, which, I now know, was born in the 1840s and, by 1866, stretched both across the American nation and the Atlantic Ocean—a rise only slightly longer than that followed by television a century later (Sconce 21).

I finished my beer, packed my belongings and my ignorance, and put the work aside for further study and future reflection.

The computer, in all its many and varied forms, has been much-studied, and I neither focus upon the computer within this collection nor speculate on its seemingly overnight rise to prominence in our professional discussions of "technology" in the classroom—a rise to the place-of-pride in our discussions just a bit longer than that followed by the telegraph, actually. The technologies that bear down upon the writing process that came before the computer have been less studied within rhetoric and composition, with considerable disconnect among the sites of study—pedagogical reflections in one set of journals, theoretical concerns in another; history of technology in one field (or subfield), history of education in another.

I offer the essays that follow as preliminary answers to a range of questions I began to formulate on the barstool in Seattle, surrounded by technologies I did not understand. Study of the computer and its place both in our world and our classrooms is important, but there are other technologies of education that once mattered—and, in many cases, may still claim some relevance to our work.

I offer the essays that follow as both introductions to the varied field that has come to be known as "technology studies" and as launching pads for further study—study, in some cases, of technologies that came onto the cultural scene, flourished within and beyond the writing classroom, and failed (either by being abandoned or replaced) without being subject to critical interrogation. In the essays that follow, essays loosely organized chronologically, a range of scholars ask and answer questions that matter about technologies that walked the cutting edge to bluntness.

The first interlocutor to step forward is Richard Leo Enos. In "Writing Without Paper: A Study of Functional Rhetoric in Ancient Athens," he argues that much of the extant writing that has been deemed worthy of study through the centuries has been writing that was *meant* to live beyond its immediate context. Here, Enos studies writing "composed for pragmatic purposes," composed for a specific audience, composed with a "goal [both] immediate and contextual."

Expanding the focus of *On the Blunt Edge,* Daniel R. Fredrick writes of other technologies fundamental to education: the technologies of transportation. In *"Adsum Magister"* Fredrick argues "the history of the literate mind—the history of rhetorical education—is caught up inextricably with the history of transportation (and all the equipment necessary for traveling)." This wide-ranging study touches upon a wide range of "inventions and infrastructures," including the leather shoe and the paved road.

Focusing on more recognizably traditional technologies of writing, Richard W. Rawnsley writes, in "Motivations for the Development of Writing Technology," that "[t]he history of writing machines *is* the history of technology, and a cutting-edge technology remains sharp for only a short time before it becomes part of the past, relegated alongside other more primitive and clumsy ways of accomplishing tasks." While the technologies he studies are more recognizable than those considered in the first two chapters, the study itself is methodically intriguing—from its careful definition of "writing machines" to its speculations about efficiency and evolution.

Like Rawnsley, Shawn Fullmer focuses upon recognizable technologies of writing in "'The Next Takes the Machine.'" Here, however, the focus turns overtly to technology and teaching. As Fullmer writes, "Documented expectations and claims about the use of the typewriter in school classrooms are evident as early as 1887." Composition as a discipline became firmly entrenched virtually concurrently with study in educational orbits—some careful and reflective, some banal and bordering on reckless—of the use of technology in teaching.

Continuing the focus upon technology and the changing practices of pedagogues, Kathleen Blake Yancey argues, in "Handwriting, Literacy, and Technology," that there are dimensions to our talk of technology that are both personal and pedagogical. She writes of handwriting, of how penmanship made her father look illiterate, of the Palmer "hand" and its value to individuals—in education and in business.

Unlike Fullmer and Yancey, Joseph Jones includes in his analysis of pedagogy a range of audio-visual aids. Most significantly, however, he writes of the ways reflective practice in the use of technology "emerged in ways in secondary schools that outpaced its emergence in

American colleges." This early emergence in the hotly contested and ever-shifting context of secondary English education led to "curricular schizophrenia."

In "Textbooks and Their Pedagogical Influences in Higher Education," Sherry Rankins Robertson and Duane Roen argue, "[t]he discipline of rhetoric and composition has used textbooks as an historical lens to retrospectively construct a theoretical overview of norms for any given time period"—from the early and limited efforts in the classical and medieval periods to the explosive growth in availability of textbooks in the nineteenth and twentieth centuries.

Continuing this focus on the textual artifacts that comprise the discipline of rhetoric and composition, Marcia Kmetz, Rob Lively, Crystal Broch, and Thomas Black review the ways discussions of technology have played out in prominent journals in rhetoric and composition. "Disciplining Technology" includes a startling range of topics, from classroom-focused discussions of dictionaries and closed-circuit TV (both in *College Composition and Communication*, both in the mid-1950s) to the phonograph (*College English*, 1939) to the stereopticon (*The English Journal*, 1912)—a sort of slide projector used primarily in military training focused on quick target identification. The computer has come to dominate our pedagogical discussions, but it is a Johnny-come-lately player in the game of the tech-savvy teaching of writing.

Broadening the focus of *On the Blunt Edge* beyond the classroom—and even the writing process as it is normally conceived within our professional discourse—Jason Thompson and Theresa Enos argue, in "The Rhetoric of Obfuscation," that our "term *palimpsest* [. . .] can be linked to ethos, a layering of texts and/or voices that can reveal our persona, character, hidden intentions." Exploring these links, Thompson and Enos rove across a range of topics, including the Archimedes codex and Da Vinci's notebooks and culminating in a five-part definition of kairotic ethos that moves our thinking about history and technology in directions both startling and productive.

The cohesiveness of the chapters that follow, the natural build of one upon the other, will be especially useful for teachers and scholars new to rhetoric and composition in general and technology studies in particular. A wide range of voices cry out from very different pieces of this wilderness. The story they tell together offers new insight into old technologies, new takes on just how broadly conceived our discussions of technology can—and should—allow themselves to be.

The story they combine to tell is one of technological innovation and achievement, mechanical failure and cultural abandonment.

The story they combine to tell is one of pedagogy and change, of practices successful and surely doomed.

The story they tell began, for me, on a barstool in Seattle, with a moment of acknowledged ignorance that led to years of study—including study of the history of paper in ancient Greece, the pedagogical system that adopted it, and the book trade that flourished in ways even the best researchers can only speculate.

Because Greece lacked the abundant deposits of clay found in the Near East, a permanent writing surface other than the clay tablet had to be devised. Wax provided only a temporary, transient surface for writing when spread within a wooden frame or series of wooden frames bound together by a leather thong, good for educational purposes but impermanent—what paleographer E. G. Turner refers to as "the apparatus of the schoolboy" (12). Leather was impractical, for the curing process that made it pliable also made it susceptible to decay, and parchment made from stretched and scraped untreated animal skins, also called vellum, was prohibitively expensive because of the time and labor involved in its manufacture. So the best alternative for the Greeks for a permanent writing surface was papyrus, although, as Herodotus suggests in the fifth century BCE, "when paper was scarce they used, instead, the skins of sheep and goats" (*V*: 314). Pliny also suggests that papyrus was the preferred writing surface when he writes that after King Ptolemy "suppressed the export of paper, parchment was invented at Pergamum" (*IV*: 70).

Although papyrus plants grew in various regions throughout Africa and the Middle East, including modern Ethiopia and Syria, the papyrus used in Greece came almost entirely from Egypt. In Egypt, particularly the Delta region of the Nile, the papyrus plant, *Cyperus papyrus*, provided a dietary supplement rich in starch; a combustible material used in smelting; a decorative material for floral displays; and a building material used for huts, boats, and furniture (Lewis 3–32). However the chief use of *Cyperus papyrus*, and certainly the most profitable, was the manufacture of paper.

As Pliny describes it in *Natural History*, written in the first century CE, the Egyptian process for making a writing surface from the papyrus plant was an art. He writes, "The process of making paper from papyrus is to split it with a needle into very thin strips made as broad as possible." These strips are laid in a vertical layer upon a board "moistened with water from the Nile," and a horizontal layer is applied over them. The two layers are pressed together, "dried in the sun and then joined together," in rolls no longer than twenty sheets (*XIII*: 72–79). Pliny also suggests these rolls were divided by quality, which may certainly be true, but other sources suggest the rolls may have either begun with a rougher, more coarse piece to provide protection when the rest of the sheets were attached and rolled, or less-than-honest dealers may have begun rolls with fine sheets and moved to sheets of progressively lower quality towards the end of the roll to dupe unsuspecting shoppers (Lewis 53–54). The size of these individual sheets varied, but the norm seems to have been for sheets roughly fourteen inches in height and nine inches in width, which allows for "a column of text between eight and ten inches high, containing between twenty-five and forty-five lines" (Reynolds and Wilson 3). Joined end-to-end with a flour paste and minimal overlap, a roll of parchment would average fifteen feet, although much larger examples exist, as do examples of rolls only a few sheets long (Casson 25).

Writing on a papyrus roll would be done in columns of eight to ten inches on the side with the horizontal strips of papyrus. As authors wrote, they would wind the text in with the left hand and wind blank papyrus out with the right, and readers would, of course, read the text in the same manner, unrolling the roll with the right hand and rolling it up with the left—as a modern reader would browse microfilm. There are two obvious disadvantages to this system of writing and reading: as a text was written or read, the beginning of that text wound deeper and deeper into the papyrus roll on the scholar's left side. When a text was completed, it had to be entirely rewound to make it ready for its next use. Every reading of a text thus involved two windings and double the wear-and-tear. Such double handling, combined with the impermanence of ink, also made it impossible to write upon both sides of the papyrus, although this was occasionally done (Reynolds and Wilson 2–4). While the damage of continuous handling must not be minimized, the fragility of these texts must not be overextended either. "It should," writes historian Naphtali Lewis, "come as no surprise to learn that papyrus books and documents had in ancient and medieval times a usable life of hundreds of years." Aristotle's manuscripts exemplify this paradoxically fragile durability, for they were part of the spoils of war taken to Rome by Sulla in 86 BCE as part of his personal loot, roughly 250 years after the original manuscripts were written (Lewis 60; Canfora 56).

For scholars, the papyrus rolls that formed books caused additional difficulties, particularly in regards to storage and access. When scholars wanted to locate a particular passage in a work, it would be necessary to unroll the papyrus until the passage was located, reread and perhaps copy the passage, and then reroll the scroll. If, as a reader was browsing a text, she wanted to mark a particular spot, she would need to place a strip of parchment on the scroll and hold it in place as she continued to roll or unroll the papyrus. To return to the marked passage, it would, of course, be necessary to subject the manuscript to yet another bout of rolling and unrolling. The wear and tear this would cause is clear, and thus it is not surprising that two scholars quoting from the same source would differ widely—even wildly—both from one another and from the original: better to rely on a sometimes faulty memory for a quotation than to move a manuscript one unroll and one reroll closer to destruction.

Storage of rolled books would be as problematic as accessing them for particular passages. Books encompassed by a single roll—such as an average Platonic dialogue—could be stored simply by rolling them, binding them closed, and setting them upon a shelf. To make locating such a book easier, a tab would often be inserted near the beginning of the scroll so that it hangs out slightly; on this tab the name of the book could be written and perhaps the name of its author. This process of placing tabs in books to identify them replaced the process of simply writing a book's title on the back of the opening page (Turner 15). Books written on multiple rolls of papyrus were more problematic. They would be rolled, bound, and marked with tabs, but they would then need to be stored together in a basket or box. The problems here concern space. Rolls stacked atop one another are difficult to separate from the pile without jostling their neighbors. Rolls resting in baskets take up a lot of space on a library's shelf, and rolls in boxes are, at the lower levels, impossible to see individually without digging through the scrolls on the top layers. As the rolls of papyrus are handled, the tabs with which they are marked drop out, making any organizational scheme laborious to maintain.

So these were the books as they existed in Aristotle's library during—and in the centuries after—his lifetime: rolls of varying lengths made from Egyptian papyrus and stacked on shelves with tabs to identify them. Writers were able to use only one side of each surface, and readers slowly destroyed their books as they read them over and over again. Of the book trade that disseminated these works throughout the ancient world, little can be said with certainty.

As Lewis writes, "[By] the sixth century [BCE] papyrus was clearly in common use in the Greek world" (87). By the time Aristotle came to Athens, in fact, a thriving trade in papyrus had developed between Egypt and Greece, and writing material was readily available to Greek scholars. Debate exists, however, regarding even the cost of papyrus and of the books ultimately written upon it, and, as Turner observes, "our ignorance of the methods of the trade is complete. All that we do know is that books are mentioned among the cargoes of ships, and that books are bought and sold in Athens" (20–21). Concerning the cost of papyrus in Greece a generation before Aristotle, historian Bill Katz writes, "Some ideas as to the cost of papyrus can be found in the fact that in the year 407 [BCE] two papyrus rolls were worth seven times as much as a day laborer's wages" (46). While this may have been the cost for complete blank rolls of papyrus of unknown quality, Plato asserts in the "Apology" that inexpensive books, probably only a few sheets of papyrus long, were available in the *agora*. He writes of the books of Anaxagoras that students "might cheaply purchase them" for a drachma and thus learn their subversion from a source other than Socrates (37). In another instance, young Phaedrus reads the words of Lysias to Socrates, words read from a borrowed book—suggesting that while valuable, the text was not considered irreplaceable by its owner (113–14).

The manner in which books spread bore no resemblance to the literary-industrial complex with which modern scholars and readers are familiar, a system predicated on a definition of a book as an object published by an author through "'an organized book trade for the benefit of an expectant public'" (qtd. in Turner 16). This is an idea born of the eighteenth and nineteenth century that simply does not apply to Greece during and after Aristotle's lifetime. For a model of how publication likely worked during this time, we turn to Isocrates.

While Isocrates was incapable of delivering his speecheshis works clearly enjoyed widespread popularity—and Aristotle clearly owned or had ready access to copies of Isocrates's work as he wrote the *Rhetoric*. The works were probably read with the borrowed voice of a student, initially. For publication, a method similar to the vanity presses may have been employed—where an author would produce, or pay to produce—multiple copies of a work, the distribution of which he or she would closely supervise. This seems to have been Isocrates's favored method, and he argues in *Antidosis* that once his work had been spread in this way he gained a widespread reputation and attracted numerous pupils. His words, he brags in the *Panathenaicus*, spread beyond Athens to Sparta through their publication (Turner 19–20).

Although Isocrates's method of publication involved much work and supervision on the part of the author, other methods of publication did exist. Copies of books were produced through the patronage of the wealthy, through the work of students, and by the efforts of early librarians and readers. The progression of this development, however, the scope of the book trade as it developed in the ancient world, is impossible to describe with certainty, although it is safe to say that in Greece during the fifth and fourth centuries BCE it is unlikely publishers existed as we know them, "that is, a person willing to take the risk of multiplying copies before it was known that there would be any public demand for the author's work" (Turner 20). What we can say with certainty is only this: "By the first thirty years of the fourth century [BCE, roughly the time of Aristotle's birth, maturation, and journey to Plato's academy], books have established themselves, and their tyranny lies ahead" (23).

The tyranny of the book continues, despite regular prophecies of doom from proponents of new technologies (and despite the fact that, at least for the first several hundred years, the printing process was dauntingly complex, expensive, difficult, labor intensive, and prone to both error and abuse—all described in detail by Alister McGrath in his history of the *King James Bible*). The tyranny of the computer within our professional discussions of "technology" continues, and calls to return to the world of pen and paper grow both infrequent and increasingly marginalized.

But tyrants come and go, as those papyrus-using, book-dealing Greeks referenced above understood well, and the ebb and flow of tyranny is as observable in technology as in politics. I offer a final example to illustrate the point, an example that exists in the wonderfully American intersection of education and administration, education and classroom teaching, corporate advertising, and technological innovation as panacea.

On my desk, not far from my much-abused copy of the *Rhetoric*, I keep a dead technological artifact that dominated personal mathematics for fifty years: a Ve-Po-Ad. It's slightly larger than a pack of cigarettes and less than half of an inch thick. The scuffed leather case flips open to reveal a brass and black face with ten columns numbered nine to zero. There are places on the face to stick a pencil tip in and manipulate the digits. My mother gave this to me some years ago, after it served her throughout junior high and high school. Manufactured by the Reliable Typewriter and Adding Machine Corporation in Chicago, it sold for just under three dollars in 1926 (Babbitts 127). The age and wear suggest it belonged either to my grandmother or great-grandmother, too, even though it came to my mother in the 1960s and to me in the 1990s.

How this oddly heavy machine works is an absolute mystery to me, although Internet research turns up many, many histories of and instructions for the Ve-Po-Ad and similar "Magic Brain Calculators"—from roughly 1917 through the 1960s. I have tried to read these instructions and follow them. I have tried to do simple arithmetic using my Ve-Po-Ad. I have failed repeatedly and consistently.

No one in the chapters that follow mentions the Ve-Po-Ad.

Every chapter that follows tells a piece of its story.

WORKS CITED

Babbitts, Judith. "Stereographs and the Construction of a Visual Culture in the United States." *Memory Bytes: History, Technology, and Digital Culture.* Ed. Lauren Rabinovitz and Abraham Geil. Durham, NC: Duke UP, 2004. 126–49. Print.

Canfora, Luciano. *The Vanished Library: A Wonder of the Ancient World.* Trans. Martin Ryle. Berkeley: U of California P, 1990. Print.

Casson, Lionel. *Libraries in the Ancient World.* New Haven, CT: Yale UP, 2001. Print.

Herodotus. *The Persian Wars V.* Trans. George Rawlinson. 9 vols. New York: Modern Library, 1942. 295–339. Print.

Katz, Bill. *Dahl's History of the Book.* 3rd ed. Metuchen, NJ: Scarecrow, 1995. Print.

Lewis, Naphtali. *Papyrus in Classical Antiquity.* Oxford: Oxford UP, 1974. Print.

McGrath, Alister. *In the Beginning: The Story of the King James Bible and How It Changed a Nation, a Language, and a Culture.* New York: Anchor, 2001. Print.

Meadow, Charles T. *Ink into Bits: A Web of Converging Media.* Lanham, MD: Scarecrow, 1998. Print.

Plato. "Apology." *Euthyphro, Apology, Crito, Phaedo.* Trans. Benjamin Jowett. Buffalo, NY: Prometheus, 1988. 27–53. Print.

—. "Phaedrus." *The Rhetorical Tradition: Readings from Classical Times to the Present.* Trans. H. N. Fowler. Ed. Patricia Bizzell and Bruce Herzberg. Boston, MA: Bedford, 1990. 113–43. Print.

Pliny. *Natural History IV.* Trans. H. Rackham. 9 vols. Cambridge, MA: Harvard UP, 1945. Print.

Reynolds, L. D., and N. G. Wilson. *Scribes and Scholars: A Guide to the Transmission of Greek and Latin Literature.* 3rd ed. Oxford: Clarendon, 1991. Print.

Sconce, Jeffrey. *Haunted Media: Electronic Presence from Telegraphy to Television.* Durham, NC: Duke UP, 2000. Print.

Turner, E. G. *Athenian Books in the Fifth and Fourth Centuries B.C.* London: Lewis, 1952. Print.

ON THE BLUNT EDGE

1 Writing Without Paper: A Study of Functional Rhetoric in Ancient Athens

Richard Leo Enos

> *From the public and private buildings in and around the Athenian market place have come thousands of informal inscriptions scratched or painted on pots or on potsherds and on other everyday objects. Beginning soon after the introduction of the alphabet into Greece (now generally agreed to be near the middle of the 8th century B.C.), these casual notations continue in ever increasing numbers up through the 6th century of our era. They range in subject matter from the simplest ABC (alpha, beta, gamma) writing exercise or the scratching of a name, whether that of the writer, a god, or a friend, to complicated messages or detailed commercial notations. Such petty communications and expressions of individuality achieve a kind of importance by virtue of their very triviality. The writers, intent on their own concerns and giving no thought to the searching eye of history, reveal themselves unselfconsciously and give us not only an insight into everyday life in each succeeding period but also pure and unadulterated evidence concerning the history of literacy (letter shapes, letter values, spelling, direction of writing, use of abbreviation, and so on). (3)*
>
> —Mabel Lang, *Graffiti in the Athenian Agora*

INTRODUCTION

Visitors to the Acropolis Museum of Athens will find three small statues of Hymettian marble, dating back to the sixth century BCE, depicting scribes with scrolls on their laps (*cf.* Paráassoglou).* These representations portray (and reinforce) our long-accepted stereotype of classical Athens as a city that prized literacy. Yet in some sense these images misdirect our view of writing in Athens, and the dimensions of what is commonly considered to be the first real literate community of Western civilization. These statues, and the masterpieces of literature that we are fortunate enough to have today, capture only the best of writing, but not the range of writing in Athens. To call Athens a "literate community" we must do her justice by exploring all the dimensions of writing . . . not only the magnificent artifacts of literary art.

Thanks to the diligence of archaeologists, and particularly the century-long painstaking efforts of The American School of Classical Studies at Athens, we have unearthed writing that was not only intended for everyday, functional rhetoric but writing that is evident in virtually every facet of daily life in Athens. The purpose of this essay is not, of course, to review the three thousand plus inscriptions that have been unearthed from the Agora excavations (Lang, *Graffiti and Dipinti* 1), although many of these invaluable inscriptions indeed merit individual study but rather to review the tendencies and practices of this civic literacy and, in that sense, help fill in the space between orality and literary masterpieces. This task is important if we hope to continue to study our history of written rhetoric in the place that first turned it into a *techne* or "art" in and of itself.

The task of generalizing about the dimensions of everyday literary practices in ancient Athens is a daunting one, particularly if we consider the "funnel effect" of research in classical rhetoric. As mentioned above, thousands of inscriptions have been unearthed, and more are discovered almost daily. These artifacts have been dutifully recorded and catalogued, primarily for the purposes of taxonomical organization. That is, the scattered array of "evidence" about writing varies with each archaeological site and, to give order to that site, classification schemes were created. Those schemes of organization, however, were never developed with the idea of studying writing habits but rather for the purposes of cataloging findings for efficient retrieval. Our purpose here will be to reexamine and, in a sense, reorder these important discoveries in order to make clear the dimensions of writing that functioned in Athens.

From such a perspective, generalizations rather than particulars are privileged. By proportion, however, few individual inscriptions have been studied, and fewer still by rhetoricians wishing to contribute to a better understanding of the history of rhetoric. The consequence of this trickle down effect is astounding: we have a wealth of primary material awaiting our attention but a paucity of scholars who are available to study them and advance cogent interpretations about their impact on the history of written rhetoric. The intent here is to offer a nascent map, a route that will help us begin the journey that leads to a much more thorough and representative understanding about rhetoric in classical Athens than exists currently. The hope driving this essay is that its contributions will quickly become outdated and replaced by more thorough and detailed research that is the result of not only a meticulous study of cataloged inscriptions but also the result of field work at Athens that will add further to our knowledge of this critical, but understudied, aspect of written rhetoric.

EVERYDAY LITERACY: A TAXONOMICAL CLASSIFICATION

Extant Athenian writings normally survived its descent through the ages because they were composed with a sense of value permanence. Written on durable material, providing information that was often intended beyond the immediate moment, their "remains" frequently were the result of a conscious intent for preservation. The writings we study here—much of which have been unearthed as recently as the last century—are uniquely different. Often composed for pragmatic purposes, their audience was specific, their goal immediate and contextual. As we can imagine, these compositions are rarely self-conscious of permanence, rarely self-reflective, and not written with the thought of being an object of study. Yet because of their very casual and (in certain instances) unabashed qualities, they candidly reveal much about daily writing practices of Athenians. Moreover, because of their functional nature, they were not written as genre, except in the loosest sense. Yet we have collected enough of these artifacts that we can begin to group these writings in order to examine their rhetorical nature and, in the process, learn much more about everyday literacy practices.

As mentioned above, the cataloguing procedures of the researchers of The American School of Classical Studies at Athens were never developed with the intent of studying rhetoric. Rather, their grouping of epigraphy was created for identification common to systems of archaeological classification. For our purposes in rhetoric, the graffiti discussed here fall into four general categories: educational practices, civic literacy, commercial transactions, and expressive writing.

EDUCATIONAL PRACTICES

Figure 1. An incomplete abecedarium, by the permission and courtesy of The American School of Classical Studies at Athens: Agora Excavations.

There are abundant examples of writing that demonstrate practice at compositional skills; often these artifacts appear as nascent efforts to learn the alphabet or abecedarium (Figure 1, Lang, *Graffiti* #1). We know that Athenians regularized their writing from left to right after 500 BCE, but there is early evidence, in some cases as early as the eighth and seventh centuries BCE, that shows such practices as not only moving from right to left but following a *boustrophedon* style; that is, writing that reverses order when reaching the end of a line so the script moves from right to left, and then from left to right and back again (Woodhead 26 *ff.*). Such early fragments are critically important for the history of rhetoric because they show that at its earliest introduction writing was a pragmatic skill that was being studied. We often think writing emerges as a craft-skill, or a technique that develops into a working profession, such as a scribe or a technographer (Enos, "Inventional"). Craft-skills clearly are apparent in Athens, for there is ample evidence about professions that came into existence for the sole purpose of writing public documents and various other forms of civic *testemonia* (Enos, "Literacy"). Here, however, we see not the efforts of professionals refining their art or craft-skill but rather efforts by early writers to master a technology for broad-based civic purposes. The inference is that writing was being learned because it functioned so well in civic matters. That is, citizens who did not see themselves as craft-specialists nonetheless recognized the advantages of learning (at least) the rudiments of composition. These forms of writing are manifested in civic practices such as we see later in this chapter.

Figure 2. Writing implements from Athens, by the permission and courtesy of The American School of Classical Studies at Athens: Agora Excavations.

Civic Literacy

Athens was inscribed with public records chronicling events and preserving memorable individuals for posterity. Yet these forms of stable literacy—or writing intended to "freeze" knowledge for posterity—only represent one aspect of civic literacy. The fragmentary inscriptions and archaeological evidence provide another important dimension to civic literacy—the kind of writing necessary for the daily activity of community life. Excavated inscriptions reveal the common practice of using *horos* stones or boundary markers. These markers functioned as location sites, much like we would use our own present-day street signs to guide us in our own communities. Often such markers, positioned prominently on the ground and standing about three feet in height, would "speak" to readers through such first person declarations as "I am the boundary stone of the Agora" (ΗΟΡΟΣ ΕΙΜΙ ΤΕΣ ΑΓΟΡΑΣ, see Lang, *Athenian Citizen* #35; Wycherley 218). *Horos* stones indicate that members of the community were literate to the extent that they could read these simple signs for purposes of direction and location.

In a similar respect, Athens used water clocks or *klepsydra* (Enos, "Inventional"). In a functional and pragmatic sense, telling time is a sort of literacy. These water clocks were used to limit the time of speech in law courts; that is, when the water ran out of the pot, the orator's time was up. There were also, however, public clocks, positioned in the Agora for easy viewing, so the community could read the clock and know the time.

Other inscriptions reveal yet another dimension of civic literacy. *Ostraka* excavated only last century reveal that voters would write down their decisions about who should be banished from the city (Broneer). As Eugene Vanderpool points out so lucidly, the fact that these original documents were written down by "average citizens" is immensely important, for by the mere number of these hundreds of examples we are able to advance some generalizations about writing habits and linguistic principles employed not by artists but by everyday practioners (227). Similarly, excavated voting tablets and ballots have the names of *demes* or parishes so a record could be kept of those who exercised their voting rights (and obligations) at any time the democracy was active. All such activities, the marking of streets, the voting inscriptions and ballots, and even the reading of time, reveal a type of functional, active literacy that helped Athens conduct her civic affairs.

Figure 3. Voting tablets with the names of famous Athenians, by the permission and courtesy of The American School of Classical Studies at Athens: Agora Excavations.

COMMERCIAL TRANSACTIONS

One of the most revealing dimensions of functional rhetoric is evident in the routine business transactions and "errands" of Athenians. In some instances they are little more than grocery lists, yet the practice is evident in Greece even before the invention of the alphabet. For example, Bronze Age Linear B tablets, currently on display at the National Archaeological Museum in Athens, provide writing that lists and records qualities of food and animal holdings (Chadwick, e.g., 118, 158-61). Writing was used initially as an aid to memory and the value of accurate economic (used here in the literal Greek sense of "house keeping") records is obvious. What is amazing is the widespread practice and familiarity of such lists. One Athenian inscription, dated to the fourth century BCE, shows how such writings were also done for social events by recording a listing of banquet items (Figure 4). Another Athenian inscription, dated even earlier in the sixth century BCE, delivers a message for couches (Lang, *Graffiti* #22). What is significant about this cryptic message is that it has a salutation of "Boy" (ΠΑΙ; see also Lang, *Graffiti and Dipinti* B2). The obvious inference here is that the "boy" performing the errand can read. Such examples as the graffiti mentioned above are offered only to illustrate the point that we can learn much from such fragmentary evidence about function, readership, and purpose involving literary practices of commercial transactions.

Figure 4. A fourth century BCE banquet list, by the permission and courtesy of The American School of Classical Studies at Athens: Agora Excavations.

EXPRESSIVE WRITING

Offering gifts with notes was a common practice among Athenians. These notes were often inscribed right on the gift itself. Frequently, such items did more than record the name of the giver; they also expressed some sentiment of love, honor, and appreciation. In short, everyday writing of this nature frequently included some expression of the author's thoughts and sentiments. We are inclined to think of such expressive writing as "love gifts" and indeed examples of such affectionate writing abounds. Yet there is also evidence of the darker side of expressive writing. Frequently, such writing also reveals emotive venting through name-calling ("X" is lustful [κατάπυγον]!; Lang, *Graffiti* #6; Lang, *Graffiti and Dipinti* C27), obscenities, visual pornography that complements the verbal, and even curses. In the following (Figure 5), Kallixenos is called a "traitor" and Themistokles is told that he should "get out" (see Lang, *Athenian Citizen* #28). One example of expressive rhetoric is especially striking: a fourth century BCE lamp has an inscription that is written backward, clearly (but consistently) in the wrong direction, prompting Lang to suggest such "wrong-way writing" may be an attempt at "black magic" (Lang, *Graffiti* #53 and accompanying text; Lang, *Graffiti and Dipinti* C32). Other inscriptions, however, leave no doubt about the author's feelings, for they call upon the worst of fates to befall their recipients. These examples reveal that such functional writing was done to convey emotions, that writing was much more than a recording and labeling device, and done to express (strongly in many cases) attitudes and dispositions.

Figure 5 "Emotive" Ostraka, by permission and courtesy of The American School of Classical Studies at Athens: Agora Excavations.

CONCLUSION

These few, isolated examples are offered to make the point of this chapter: fragmentary evidence of commonplace, functional rhetoric offers insights to the wide range of literary practices in ancient Athens. Earlier work, as cited above and as offered in the accompanying bibliography of this essay, has already clearly established that writers—ranging from artisans who inscribed public monuments to court reporters—represented established writing trades within Athenian society. The evidence of graffiti discussed here, however, focuses on nonprofessional writers. This mundane, but candid, everyday evidence illustrates the range of common writing practices among nonprofessional, but clearly literate, Athenians. Such writings reveal, in the most general but important sense, that writing and reading were pervasive throughout virtually every aspect of Athenian society. Such a range of literary practice prompts us to extend our praise of Athens as a society that not only prized artistic literacy but also for a society that practiced functional literacy on a daily basis.

ACKNOWLEDGMENTS

This essay is dedicated to my first teacher of epigraphy, Fordyce W. Mitchell, and to Mabel Lang, whose pioneering work made this study possible.

The figures presented in this essay are referenced in the following works. I wish to thank Jan Jordan, Secretary of the Agora Excavations, and The American School of Classical Studies at Athens, for securing permission to use the official photographs that appear in the works listed here: Fig. 1: Lang, Mable. *Graffiti in the Athenian Agora*. Princeton, New Jersey: The American School of Classical Studies at Athens, 1974, #1 (A2 P6074, P3272). Fig. 2: Thompson, Dorothy Burr. *The Athenian Agora: An Ancient Shopping Center*. Princeton, New Jersey: The American School of Classical Studies at Athens, 1971, #46. Fig. 3: *The Athenian Agora: A Guide to the Excavation and Museum*. Revised fourth edition. The American School of Classical Studies at Athens. Princeton, New Jersey: Institute for Advanced Study, 1990, #155, p. 256. Fig. 4: Lang, Mabel. *Graffiti in the Athenian Agora* #49 (B12). Fig. 5: Lang, Mabel. *The Athenian Citizen*. Princeton, New Jersey: The American School of Classical Studies at Athens, 1960, #28.

WORKS CITED

The Athenian Agora: A Guide to the Excavation and Museum. Rev. 4th ed. The American School of Classical Studies at Athens. Princeton, NJ: Institute for Advanced Study, 1990. Print.

Broneer, Oscar. "Excavations on the North Slope of the Acropolis, 1937." *Hesperia* 7 (1938): 161–263. Print.

Chadwick, John. *The Decipherment of Linear B.* 2nd ed. Cambridge: Cambridge UP, 1970. Print.

Enos, Richard Leo. "Inventional Constraints on the Technographers of Ancient Athens: A Study in *Kairos*." *Rhetoric and Kairos: Essays in History, Theory, and Praxis.* Ed. Phillip Sipiora and James S. Baumlin. Albany, NY: SUNY P, 2002. 77–88. Print.

—. "Literacy in Athens During the Archaic Period: A Prolegomenon to Rhetorical Invention." *Perspectives on Rhetorical Invention.* Ed. Janet M. Atwill and Janice M. Lauer. Tennessee Studies in Literature, Volume 39. Knoxville: U of Tennessee P, 2002. 176–91. Print.

Lang, Mabel. *Graffiti and Dipinti. The Athenian Agora: Results of the Excavations Conducted by The American School of Classical Studies at Athens,* Volume XXI. Princeton, NJ: The American School of Classical Studies at Athens, 1976. Print.

—. *The Athenian Citizen.* Princeton, NJ: The American School of Classical Studies at Athens, 1960. Print.

—. *Graffiti in the Athenian Agora.* Princeton, NJ: The American School of Classical Studies at Athens, 1974. Print.

Paráassoglou, G. M. "A Roll Upon His Knees." *Yale Classical Studies* 28: *Papyrology* (1985): 273–75. Print.

Vanderpool, Eugene. "Ostracism at Athens. I. The Ostraca. II. Some Historical Points." *Lectures in Memory of Louise Taft Semple.* University of Cincinnati Classical Studies Series 2. Ed. C. G. Boulter, et al. Norman: U of Oklahoma P for the University of Cincinnati, 1973: 215–70. Print.

Woodhead, A. G. *The Study of Greek Inscriptions.* Cambridge: Cambridge UP, 1967. Print.

Wycherley, R. E. *Literary and Epigraphical Testimonia. The Athenian Agora: Results of the Excavations Conducted by The American School of Classical Studies at Athens,* Volume III. Princeton, NJ: The American School of Classical Studies at Athens, 1957. Print.

2 *Adsum Magister:* The Technology of Transportation in Rhetorical Education

Daniel R. Fredrick

> *There is a peculiar fluidity about secondary education in Hellas: the teachers are always on the move [. . .] Their pupils had either to follow them abroad, as Isokrates went to Gorgias in Thessaly, or wait for their next visit.*
>
> —Kenneth J. Freeman

> *There are 745 million schoolchildren in the world, and getting to class is a universal problem.*
>
> —Wilfred Owen

THE PROBLEM

We can imagine: if Gorgias has the leg power to walk from Leontini to Syracuse (about twenty-two miles), he then needs to find a vessel to carry him about five hundred miles over the sea to the Greek port of Piraeus. After disembarking in Piraeus, Gorgias then must finish off the journey with a six-mile walk to Athens. His students as well will need to travel in order to meet him wherever he chooses to lecture, in the city center or the house of Callicles. If Gorgias never arrives at Athens, it is difficult to determine when or whether persuasion-hungry Athenians will ever learn the Gorgianic figures or how to speak extemporaneously on any topic. To be sure, in all times and in all cultures, it is imperative that student and teacher converge in some environment.

14

Just as the Greek alphabet, a technology, helped the ancients traverse from an oral state of mind to a literate state of mind,[1] so too did advances in the technology of transportation help bards, sophists, and students traverse the rocky terrain of Greece and billowing seas of the Mediterranean in order to unite with a wider audience whom they could teach or from whom they could learn. In the history of rhetorical education, this unification is one of the greatest necessities and poses one of schooling's greatest challenges, far greater perhaps than the challenge of stoking zeal for learning or enhancing aptitude. As Wilfred Owen implies in the epitaph above, getting students to school is no trivial matter; there needs to be sound infrastructure and accouterments of travel (86). Unquestionably, the history of the literate mind—the history of rhetorical education—is caught up inextricably with the history of transportation (and all the equipment necessary for traveling) whether it means getting the student to the teacher, the teacher to the student, or both to a common locality.

In this essay, I discuss the manners in which students got (and get) to school and the inventions and infrastructure that aided them. All of these inventions for getting to school, and getting to school more easily—most of them thousands of years in use (things such as the shoe and the mile marker)—may not seem as astounding or impressive as Segwaysâ and rocket fuel (or rocket fuel combustion), but they are critically important in the history of rhetorical education, toward the final goal of producing, prolonging, and promoting literacy and training students to be ethically mindful citizens communicating artfully and appropriately.

HOME SCHOOL

In the ancient world, the teacher/student convergence was only possible face-to-face because of the oral nature of instruction. Today, face-to-face teaching is still the norm in pedagogical practice, but we have, in the digital age, variations and alternatives on the method: variations when our faces appear in a montage of electronic pixels (web conferencing, *iChat*, etc.); alternatives when we can do long distance learning via email, web pages, instant messaging, and television (community access channels etc.). In order for the educative process to occur (no matter what the medium), three elements—the student, the teacher, and the facility—must converge. Before there were traveling sophists and permanent school locations such as Plato's Academy and Aristotle's Lyceum, education took place in the home (Smith 185). The teachers were *pater* and *mater*, and their children, the students. Students learned what today we would deem as the practical arts: cooking, personal finance, tilling the fields, milking, planting, and harvesting. They would also learn *pankration* skills, such as wrestling and boxing for military duties and weapon use to protect the home. A young man was equally skilled with the plow and the sword. In Rome particularly, ancient homes emphasized what modern homeschool education still emphasizes: lessons in morality and duty to elders and gods—in a word, Roman piety. Lessons in literacy were also a long part of the ancient homeschooling curriculum. Socrates, for instance, had fond memories of his mother reading fables to him (Connolly 33).

Getting to school in this early era, it goes without saying, poses no problem. Each element—student, teacher, facility—converge naturally in the domicile. However, newer pedagogical paradigms, such as those brought to Athens by itinerant sophists, eventually vied for chief authority over educating young minds. There occurred, consequently, an inevitable break in homeschooling as sophists gave lessons in molding "capable statesmen" outside the home (Marrou 47).

School Outside the Home

Once the itinerant sophist attracted attention throughout Greece, enticing young students who were charmed by his clever, radical, and innovative oratory, the problem of getting to school, that is, to the sophist's lectures, became the burden of the student. The *pater familias*, in order to keep up with the changing times and the new rhetorical demands required of citizens in democracies, had to surrender his authority (and wallet) to the sophist. This new paradigm—administered outside the home—split the familial-pedagogical relationship between parent and child. Why should this be noteworthy? There were two dangerous costs. The first is often noted in the history books, that the father could no longer directly supervise the moral teachings of his children. The second is seldom noted, that travel in the ancient world exposed students to muggers and murderers while on the road. Leaving home meant entering the wilderness.

Outside the ancient city wall of Rome, for example, which encircled and insulated the inhabitants, was the "Abode of the dead"

(Perrottet 59). Tombstones—not convenience stores—line the *Via Appia*. The *Via Mortis* would not have been an inappropriate alternative name. The sea too, an even fiercer wilderness than the road, was another obstacle for traveling students. Pirates were real threats, and Neptune's violent waves were grave dangers. The danger of travel was not so remarkable of course when a student only needed to walk to a city center, specifically to the *trivium*, the intersection of the three roads where many grammar and rhetoric teachers held class. Yet when "study abroad" began in the classical world and became a tradition in liberal education, students had to prepare themselves for long distance travel. Indeed, by the sixteenth century, according to Comenius, studying abroad was deemed as the fourth and final stage of schooling (Cole 338). [2] Whether the student was headed toward the city center or some other school farther away, the first step outside the home required foot protection.

THE SHOE

Anthrokinetic power, the use of the body to propel the body, was the foremost means of transportation in early rhetorical education, and the foot is a major factor in this activity. The foot, as Otis Tufton Mason perceptively describes in *Primitive Travel and Transportation*, is shaped like a tripod with the ball of the heel, the end of the arch, and the toes serving as the three points of contact to the ground (257). Continually hitting the ground and enduring great pressure, the foot is one of the most vulnerable parts of the body. The foot needs protection. Among the Greeks, only the Spartans—notoriously severe—demanded barefootedness a part of their pedagogy (Graves 151). The military goals of the Spartans were designed to toughen every part of the Spartan warrior, including his feet. No matter what the weather or terrain or debris on the ground, Spartan students could not wear shoes. In contrast, the Athenians did not feel blistered feet helped one in democratic business. The Athenians were thus far better stewards of the foot than the Spartans, making shoe production into an art. The presence of the cobbler was in fact strong in the *agora*. His shops would have emitted pungent odors, and clouds from his tanning chemicals would have tainted the entire shopping area (Buford 21).

The shoe was not invented solely for getting students to school. Nevertheless, a good shoe was necessary for students as cities expanded and the grounds of city centers were littered with all sorts of things that could injure or infect the foot—cold temperatures, broken glass, chariot wheels, animal feces, and even human feces indifferently discarded out of apartment windows. Xenophon notes that "the average Athenian spent all his time upon his legs: to sit down was the mark of a slave. He walked nearly all day" (Freeman 141). This continual abuse to the foot, as Mason explains, would have led artisans to give special attention to the sole of the shoe (311). In addition to paying a cobbler to fasten together the best pieces of leather, ancient students, after a rigorous or long journey, would have rubbed down the soles of their (clean) bare feet with butter, an ointment for blisters and corns (Woods and Woods 33). As the shoe is an important accessory of travel, there was a corollary between "improvements in foot travel" and "improvements in footwear" such as better leather and stitching (Woods and Woods 18). To us, a leather shoe and good sole sparks little fascination, but imagine the response to a shoe made of Greek leather from the ancient Egyptians who walked around in shoes made of laced papyrus (like wrapping feet in braided corn husks)—which were designed primarily to shield the soft flesh of the foot from burning sand and scorpion tails (Ferris, et al. 12–13).

THE PROCESSION

Shoes will protect the feet, but what will protect the student? The Greeks and Romans, as did the Chinese, invented a processional for getting to school. Although students were relatively safe inside the city walls, young people in all cultures need supervision, both to keep them safe from trouble and to prevent them from perpetrating trouble. For this reason, walking to and from school in the dark was forbidden and so was walking alone (Connolly 34). One of the most interesting characters of rhetorical history, the one assigned the task of protecting and orchestrating students on the way to school, was the *paidagogos*. The *paidagogos*, a servant of the house, was a "mixture of nurse, footman, chaperon, and tutor," who superintended the processional to school (Freeman 66). In the following passage, the poet Lucian colorfully records the Roman student's walk to school:

> He gets up at dawn, washes the sleep from his eyes, and puts on his cloak. Then he goes out from his father's house, with his eyes fixed upon the ground, not looking at anyone who

meets him. Behind him follow attendants and *paidagogoi*, bearing in their hands the implements of virtue, writing-tablets or books containing the great deeds of olds, or, if he is going to a music-school, his well-tuned lyre.[3] (Freeman 79)

As well as a security benefit, there was a pedagogical benefit to the procession. The procession allowed the student some time to prepare himself mentally for the rigors of the school day. We can imagine the *paidagogoi* chanting Latin and Greek verb endings (in every tense and every mood) with the children. Donning the proper clothing also helped the student take on the proper persona of a student—methodical, obedient, and respectful. Frank Pierrepont Graves notes that in China, during the Confucian era, the school procession was set up to be a meaningful transition from home to school. Students donned "fest garb and tasseled cap[s]" (65). We can infer here from the ancient processionals that every day of school and every part of school—even getting to school—was meaningful. This whole idea of an organized procession to school was one of the many ancient inventions related to school travel, long before bus routes, fire escape routes, assigned seating, and any other methods for systematizing the movement of students.

The processions to school were important when schools were located within a short walking distance, that is, when school locations were fixed—such as Isocrates's house or Plato's garden, two schools that beckoned pupils "from all parts of the civilized world" (Freeman 180). Nevertheless when students began to travel greater distances and between cities, and later between countries, the procession became obsolete and the student going to school was just one among many kinds of travelers on the road—traders, soldiers, pilgrims (perhaps going to the *Panhellenic* games), the sick on their way to the island of Kos to the main temple of Asclepius, [4] oracle seekers on the way to Delphi, government officials, *proxenos*, and even tourists (Casson, *Everyday Life* 111–112). Indeed, the road is one of the key parts of the infrastructure for travel, an invention that spawns innumerable other inventions that aid students in traversing the Earth to seek out wisdom just as merchants would seek out olive oil or marble coffins.

STUDENTS ON GREEK PASSAGEWAYS:
WALKING STICKS AND DONKEYS

Freeman notes above that ancient Greek students from all over the Hellenic world, especially Attica and the Peloponnese, would travel to the schools of Isocrates and Plato (190). [5] But Greece's rough landscape made getting to school hard work. Much of the terrain in Greece is better suited for olives and cloven hooves of hill dwelling beasts rather than bipedal travelers. The roots of olive trees can sturdy themselves in the cracks of the stony topography, but on rocky terrain the human foot slips and wobbles. Three legs—the minimum needed for balance—are a great advantage. It is no surprise then that one of the corollary inventions of getting to school is the walking stick, or staff. Interestingly, the staff to the Greek student would have been much more useful than the wheel (James and Thorpe 51), but there was an even better alternative for getting along in Greece. Pausanius, famous for writing what amounts to the first archeological guide, notes that the laborious road to Delphi was best traversed with a pack animal such as a donkey (Casson, *Travel* 52–68). [6] Walking staffs and donkey paths indeed alleviated some of the problems of traveling in Greece. Yet the hilly terrain never deterred students from studying oratory there, for it was known that the strenuous walks fostered natural talent in oratory because all the stepping up and climbing down strengthened the lungs of roving orators and brought about, in the days before amplifiers, that fundamental virtue in public speaking: vociferation.

Though the donkey was better suited to travel in Greece than other vehicles, Greece was not fully bereft of a road system. Lionel Casson explains that roads gradually improved and that in place was a dual track system, which allowed an *apene*, a mule cart, moving in the opposite direction to pass, a primitive version of a modern railroad track. This dual track system was effective especially en route to sacred places, locales that merited sound upkeep. It was, possibly, on a dual track where Odysseus came head on with his father between Delphi and Thebes, both men resisting to yield the passing track, and thus, in a moment of ancient road rage, fought till death (68–70). Still, a simple road, flat, straight, wide, covering over thirty thousand miles by the middle of the Empire—like Rome's *Via Appia*—would have been a welcome invention for students and teachers throughout Greece, but was impossible because of the uneven landscape (Friedlander 268–280). In contrast, Rome's topography was better suited for a road.

STUDENTS ON ROMAN ROADS: THE *VIA APPIA*

By 140 AD, about three hundred years after the first stone was laid on the *Via Appia*, Aristides remarked that the ease of travel was one of Rome's greatest achievements (Perrottet 14). Indeed, the Roman roads, because they had very few curves, increased travel speeds immensely (Casson, *Travel* 166). A donkey, moving along a Greek road, is steady-footed but unhurried. On the right kind of paved material such as that used for the *Via Appia*, however, humans could move along at impressive speeds (for only having two legs). Ludwig Friedlander calculates that Caesar got from Rhone to Rome in eight days, marching in military procession more than fifty miles a day with gear and vehicles and animals (280). Couriers, also moving briskly along the road, would not have been much faster than Caesar's war caravan.

But the *Via Appia* itself—though constructed with engineering precision, and though superior to a donkey trail and more predictable and navigable than the seas—did not aid the convergence of students and teachers so much as the corollary inventions that it spawned. If we judge the road by its primary purpose—to quicken the pace of travel—it fell short in its ability to eliminate the dangers involved in student traveling, for the road is not partial: robbers and murderers too can speed up. To see the road as an actual asset in the history of rhetorical education, we must associate it with those road-related inventions that fostered a student's *safe* travel. The list is impressive: maps, travel guides, mile markers, hostels, tollbooths, customs, international currency (and language), and various types of vehicles.

Though soldiers would have weapons, allowing them worry-free travel at night, students and other unarmed travelers would have moved along the road only during daylight. Not only was daylight useful for safety but, as there were no addresses on Roman lodgings and no public inns, it was also useful for finding one's way around a town in search for privately run room and board. During the day, mile markers as well would be more visible. Just as on today's highways one can find markers for food and gas exits, so too on the Roman road the student could find markers approximating the distance to the next town for food and sleeping quarters, all of which were usually spaced about twenty-five miles apart (Casson, *Travel* 185). Once a student stopped for the night, he checked in to a hostel that was less comfortable than even the worst of apartments in Rome's city center. In fact, most references to ancient lodgings and the innkeepers who hosted them were damning. Dora Jane Hamblin and Mary Jane Grunsfeld offer this lurid picture of a night's stay along the *Via Appia*:

> The house-keepers "doubled as prostitutes" and the owners wife was "tarred with the brush" so visitors would know to keep hands off. The beds and "pillows [were] stuffed with reeds instead of feathers, of filthy sleeping pallets crawling with fleas and bedbugs. Lizards and spiders dropped from the rafters onto guests. Bad smells swirled from both kitchen and toilet; gusts of smoke smarted the eyes." (58–59)

Students from exceptionally wealthy families were able to avoid these hellholes, not by paying for more luxurious accommodations (there weren't any), but by staying in the family mansions along the *Via Appia*. When Marcus Tullius Cicero's son, Marcus, was on route to Athens, for example, he may have stopped at one or more of his father's houses (Hamblin and Grunsfeld 65). Students, however, would not have been able to, once out of the mansion and on the road, carry on with ostentation, for the road is a hard place. We can imagine students carrying a modest sized tote for currency and travel documents, and food and water, a great contrast to the traveling entourage of Roman Emperors. Nero, for example, moved through the wilds of the open road as a way to flaunt his wealth. Friedlander writes that "Nero had a suite of a thousand carriages; his mules had silver shoes, his muleteers scarlet liveries, his outriders and runners were gorgeously clad; Poppaea [Nero's wife] had her horses harnessed with gold, and had 500 asses with her, so as to bathe in their milk every day" (288). An Empress bathing in animal milk is quite a contrast to a student flicking fleas off pajamas.

STUDY ABROAD

Yet getting to Athens to study was worth several nights in these revolting conditions, for a young Roman's education, according to the temperament of the educated class, was not fully recognized until the student spent two years studying in Athens (Daly 41). As

Tony Perrottet explains, "The city [Athens] was a high-class finishing school for every young man of breeding—a place to polish one's Greek, absorb the higher culture, network with other young scions [. . .]" (125). Is it possible to know who were the first "young scions" to study abroad? According to Lloyd W. Daly, Julius Caesar and Marcus Tullius Cicero were, surprisingly, the first students to travel with the sole purpose of formal learning (46). True enough, Greek and Roman philosophers, as far back in Greek history as Herodotus and as late in Roman history as Marcus Aurelius, "led a migratory life" and most of them "spent all their days traveling" (Friedlander 317). This traveling, though educational, was often more for historical and personal research or political reasons. Daly argues that Crassus and Antonius, heroes of Cicero's rhetorical work *De Oratore*, studied in Greece as a side issue to their primary political business (45). It was not until Caesar and Cicero journeyed to Athens and Rhodes for no other reason than to bolster their rhetorical education by studying things such as declamation, acting, and voice training that study abroad began. The study abroad movement continued long after Cicero and Caesar's generation, decreasing to some extent under the Roman Empire because Rome itself—not Athens—became the intellectual center (Daly 57). In the history of students getting to school, the *Via Appia* was only a part, however; as students came to the last rock in the *Via Appia*, finishing their land travel, they would then begin the most dangerous part of the itinerary: riding Neptune's great ocean in a sailing vessel.

SEA TRAVEL

To get from Rome to Athens by land in the ancient world was not viable. One would need to go north through Italy, then turn south for hundreds of miles down around what is now the Slovenian, Croatian, Bosnian, Serbian, and Albanian shores of the Adriatic. Sea travel was easier and, propelled by the winds, a ship was much faster than any land vehicle. Riding the water was the fastest available travel at the time, yet it was also the most potentially dangerous (White 131). Like air travel, or traveling in any public vehicle where one relies on others to drive, students—while on the seas—could not rely on their own abilities to avoid problems and take cover during inclement weather. On land, problems are often foreseeable: one can dodge hooded figures in the distance, fight off human and animal attacks, and evaluate the sky for looming storms. On the sea though, the student is at the mercy of nature. Shipwrecks in the ancient world were not unusual, and were never salvageable (Casson, *Travel* 156). Even if there were a coast guard for rescue missions, a rescue boat would need a crew of rowers to get to sinking ships, that is, if the station could even receive distress signals. Once on the water, the ship was alone, like a capsule adrift in space with no radio. A. J. Parker catalogues, through archeological remains, over twelve hundred sunken vessels (so far found) in and around the Mediterranean (5). Enormous rocks along the coast, sandy shores, and powerful squalls—these were the elements that could easily smash and sink Greek and Roman sailing ships (1).

To raise the odds of evading shipwrecks, students, along with anyone traveling, followed rituals and procedures. Greek and Roman sailing rituals would strike us today as bizarre, yet when we think of the lack of emergency equipment—no radar, no radio, no coast guard, no helicopters, no waterproof flashlights, no plastic bags, no flares, no life jackets (other than a type of swimming belt, a "leather tube filled with cork")—we can understand the desire to do anything to comfort the soul (Woods and Woods 88). What were these rituals? First, there were the ill-fated sailing dates. Any ship setting sail on Friday the thirteenth, August twenty-fourth, October fifth or November eighth—or any last day of the month—was believed to meet a catastrophic end. On these ill-omened days, all the docks were closed. Then there were the sacrifices and the omens and the dreams of the captains, any one of which, if something went wrong, would cancel the departure. The superstitions went as far as a crew member sneezing at the wrong time, or crows appearing in the rigging, or wreckage (from a previous disaster) washing up on shore, or the captain having a nightmare (Casson, *Travel* 155).

Getting approval to board a sailing ship was just as unpredictable as a crow showing up in the rigging. Because of harsh water and weather, ships sailed the Mediterranean only between May and October—and only on days when the wind was favorable to a particular craft. When the winds were accommodating, both long ships (*triremes*) and round ships (*corbitae*) could speed along impressively. On a voyage in 50 BCE, Cicero—most likely sailing on a merchant round ship, a *corbita*, the name meaning "basket"—made it to Brundisium (where the *Via Appia* ends on the back of the "heel" of Italy's boot) from Actium (on the west side of Greece with its port in the Ionian sea) in just over two weeks, and would have been there sooner if not for a layover in Corcyra because of a storm that took the lives of those who set sail a day or two earlier (Culver 42). When the winds were good and the omens augured success and security, students still had much work to do in finding a ship and getting aboard. Perrottet clarifies that in the classical world, "There were no scheduled passenger services. [. . .] Travelers had to make private arrangements" (190). To find a *gubernator*, the captain of the ship, the student "strolled up and down the dock [. . .] trying to assess which boat was most sound, most comfortable, and most favorably omened" (191). Casson enlivens this undertaking for us:

> He then transferred [. . .] to a waterfront inn or to the house of some friend who lived near the harbor. Here he stood by with his ears cocked for the cry of a herald making the rounds to announce the departure of his vessel. He had to do it this way because ships never left on a fixed schedule. First they had to await the arrival of a wind from the right quarter. Then there was the matter of the omens. (*Travel* 155)

Passport and currency in hand, the student who found a ship could then board, enter a basic cabin "just a few square feet of space that offered a place to sleep," and, during the whole trip, nervously inspect the horizon for pirates (Casson, *Travel* 66, 94). The best parts of sea travel were undoubtedly having access to the ship's hearth for hot drinks and meals and seeing the sunlit port of the destined city or, if landing at night, seeing the enormous baskets of fire functioning as lighthouses (Woods and Woods 70). At the port, the student then needed to harness a donkey, find a walking stick, and again begin land journey. Until the steam engine, the walked road and the wind-sailed sea were the chief modes of transportation for students getting to school.

MODERN TIMES

Land travel did not change much until the industrial revolution. Centuries passing, the horse eventually replaced ancient vehicles such as the *carruca* (covered wagons), the palanquin (carrying chairs) and the litter. [7] But the two most important inventions in travel were over a thousand years later: steam and the screw (Dunbar 7). The steam locomotive greatly increased the speed of land travel, and the screw changed sea travel, making it possible for ships to increase in size and, more amazingly, submerge (De Bono 14). Yet neither steam nor the screw impacted the way students got to school, for the railroad was primarily a means for transporting goods and there are, as far as I know, no submarine universities.

In the nineteenth century, and even before 1920, students were still walking or riding horses to rural school locations (Owen 86). One would think the mass production of the automobile would have influenced student travel, allowing students to drive into neighboring cities or even cross state lines to attend school. The impact of the automobile of course is immeasurable, but what really influenced the movement of students in modern times was the postsecondary schooling opportunities for the middle class: in Joliet, Illinois, around 1901, the first community college started; in 1920 the American Association of Junior Colleges was established; and today there are over one thousand community colleges in the United States. Combine the community colleges with the technical colleges and state universities and what we have is a major transformation from live-in colleges to commuter colleges. These colleges attract working students, and thus campuses need parking lots more than and instead of dorms.

One fascinating feature of the modern college in contrast with the ancient world is that some schools are so large that students need to have a means of transportation within the campus. University shuttle systems loop around the campus for those who live in the vicinity, and pass through the campus for students traveling to different buildings. Indeed, cars, motorcycles, busses, shuttles, and even bikes are central for modern education (as is gasoline, oil, etc.) (Owen 93). One cannot forget too the airplane, or should I say, affordable airfares—especially for American students—for reinstating the program of studying abroad. Jet travel allows students from around the world to experience other cultures. Before affordable air travel, students could access other worlds only through books. And, because modern education emphasizes the importance of current events and the language of the business world, getting students to the United States is now as important as it was in ancient times to get students to Rome or Athens (87).

The newest method of getting students to school—online education—relies on the computer, but this essay focuses on pre-computer technology. In spite of this focus, it is worthwhile to note that the television was the first piece of technology to enable teachers and students to teach and learn—but never meet. In 1953, the University of Houston taught the first college TV course. The separation of student and teacher would carry on. Faces would become unnecessary. The Coastline Community College, started in 1976, has no physical campus, for example. Then the ultimate 'disappearance' of the campus and teacher began when the University of Phoenix offered complete degrees online in 1989, and six years later, the Virginia Commonwealth University offered professional degrees.

The modern technological progress is astonishing, and there should be no doubt that Cicero would have emailed his son Marcus or his best friend Atticus had he a computer. Yet the ancients, I feel, would urge us to question whether the convergence of student and a live mentor is an integral part of education, just as being on the spot where Caesar was assassinated (now an X in the street near a trolley track) is integral to experiencing a lesson in the life of Caesar. Thus, I feel it is safe to assume the computer will not replace the traditional convergence of teacher, student, and facility, for we are "bound to wander over the earth like beasts in quest for food and shelter"—and education (Zweder von Martels xi). Although students, seeking education, and teachers, seeking students, will wander the roads of electricity in cyber space in the future, they will never stop wandering the seas, the skies, and the roads and highways made of stone.

NOTES

1. Walter Ong's terms in *Orality and Literacy.*

2. The first three are grammar, logic, and rhetoric, or the *trivium.*

3. Aristophanes in the *Clouds* describes the procession in nearly the same way, but quips the boys had no overcoats when it was snowing (Freeman 72).

4. Seneca, interestingly, went to Egypt for a respiratory problem (Perrottet 261).

5. Freeman tells us that students in Crete were trained like those in Sparta (32).

6. Pliny the Elder acerbically recommends mixing wine with a mule's water to stop it from kicking and preventing other traveling nuisances (Firestone 28).

7. The litter was never a student mode of travel because it required eight servants to carry it and was more suited for the pampered Roman rich who preferred beach walks but not sand in their feet. The Greeks rebuked traveling by litter because it "smacked of ostentation," reserving it only for women and invalids (Casson, *Travel* 67).

WORKS CITED

American Association of Community Colleges. American Association of Community Colleges, 2011. Web. 13 Mar 2011.

Buford, Alison. *Craftsmen in Greek and Roman Society.* London: Thames and Hudson, 1972. Print.

Casson, Lionel. *Travel in the Ancient World.* Baltimore, MD: The Johns Hopkins UP, 1994. Print

—. *Everyday Life in Ancient Rome.* Baltimore, MD: The Johns Hopkins UP, 1975. Print.

Cole, Luella. *A History of Education: Socrates to Montessori.* New York: Holt, Rinehart, and Winston, 1950. Print

Connolly, Peter. *The Ancient City: Life in Classical Athens and Rome.* Oxford: Oxford UP, 1998. Print.

Culver, Henry B. *The Book of Old Ships: From Egyptian Galleys to Clipper Ships.* New York: Dover Publications, 1992. Print.

Daly, Lloyd W. "Roman Study Abroad." *The American Journal of Philology* 71.1 (1950): 40–58. Print.

De Bono, Edward. *Eureka!: How and When the Greatest Inventions Were Made.* New York: Holt, Rinehart, and Winston, 1974. Print.

Dunbar, Seymour. *A History of Travel in America.* New York: Tudor Publishing Company, 1937. Print.

Ferris, Julie, Sue Nichoson, Jonathan Stroud, and Sally Tagholm. *Everyday Life in the Ancient World.* New York: Kingfisher, 2002. Print.

Firestone, Harvey S. *Man on the Move: the Story of Transportation.* New York: G.P. Putnam, 1967. Print.

Freeman, Kenneth J. *Schools of Hellas: an Essay on the Practice and Theory of Ancient Greek Education from 600 to 300 BC.* New York: Macmillan and Co., 1907. Print.

Friedlander, Ludwig. *Roman Life and Manners under the Early Empire.* Trans. Leonard Magnus. 4 vols. New York: Barnes and Noble, 1968. Print.

Graves, Frank Pierrepont. *A History of Education before the Middle Ages.* New York: The Macmillan Co., 1910. Print.

Hamblin, Dora Jane, and Mary Jane Grunsfeld. *The Appian Way, a Journey.* New York: Random House, 1974. Print.

James, Peter, and I. J. Thorpe. *Ancient Inventions.* New York: Ballantine, 1994. Print.

Marrou. H. I. *A History of Education in Antiquity.* Trans. George Lamb. Madison: U of Wisconsin P, 1956. Print.

Mason, Otis Tufton. *Primitive Travel and Transportation.* Washington: Government Printing Office: Smithsonian Institution United States National Museum, 1896. Print.

Ong, Walter. *Orality and Literacy: the Technologizing of the Word*. New York: Methuen and Co., 1982. Print.

Owen, Wilfred. *Transportation and World Development*. Baltimore, MD: The Johns Hopkins UP, 1987. Print.

Parker, A. J. *Ancient Shipwrecks of the Mediterranean and the Roman Provinces*. Ed. David P. Davison. Oxford: British Archaeological Reports International / Hadrian Books, 1992. Print.

Perrottet, Tony. *Pagan Holiday: On the Trail of Ancient Roman Tourists*. New York: Random House, 2003. Print.

Smith, William A. *Ancient Education*. New York: Philosophical Library, 1955. Print.

von Martels, Zweder. Introduction: The Eye and the Eye's Mind. Ed. Zweder von Martels. *Travel Fact and Travel Fiction: Studies on Fiction, Literary Tradition, Scholarly Discovery and Observation in Travel Writing*. Leiden: E.J. Brill, 1994. Print.

White, K. D. *Greek and Roman Technology*. Ithaca, NY: Cornell UP, 1984. Print.

Woods, Michael, and Mary B. Woods. *Ancient Transportation: from Camels to Canals*. Minneapolis, MN: Runestone Press, 2000. Print.

3 Motivations for the Development of Writing Technology

Richard W. Rawnsley

Most composition teachers feel strongly about the writer's tools. This is due, in part, to the fact that they obviously feel strongly about writing, or they would not be teaching it. Writing teachers tend to have done their college work in one of three subdisciplines: literature, creative writing, or composition and rhetoric. All three of these areas develop an appreciation for the written word and its importance to society, culture, and the individual. It is natural, then, for writing teachers to appreciate the technology that allows humans to communicate vicariously through time without the necessity of presence.

This appreciation for the technology of writing tends to place writing technology on a very special pedestal. This appreciation is deserved because writing technology, if properly utilized, allows us to write more with less drudgery and better quality. However, this esthetic appreciation of writing technology tends to hide the true roots of the development of writing technology. Writing technology did not develop as a result of benevolent and philanthropic purposes, but was the result of market conditions that stimulated creative minds to develop ever more productive ways to write and reproduce written material for profit. Understanding the true stimuli for the development of writing technology helps us better see the eventual benefits it holds for our students. Writing machines (including computer aided systems) are valuable as tools but not solutions to the difficulties writing teachers experience.

THE TRANSITORY NATURE OF TECHNOLOGY

The history of writing machines *is* the history of technology, and a cutting-edge technology remains sharp for only a short time before it becomes part of the past, relegated alongside other more primitive and clumsy ways of accomplishing tasks. Despite this, new technologies have a deceptive sense of immediacy that obscures their backgrounds, development, and decrepit futures. Generally, what seems remarkable and new is really the current point of a long line of development—a point that quickly becomes, if not obsolete, archaic. Computers and computer programs are a good example of this obsolescence. The personal computers of ten years ago cannot compare to the present generation in terms of memory or operating speeds or price. The extended memory of today's machines alone allows personal computers to run programs that needed mainframes in the past. Surely another ten years will take a similar toll on today's equipment.

PRINTING'S CONTRIBUTIONS TO COMPUTER WORD PROCESSING

The fast-paced changes in writing systems that we currently see began over two hundred years ago with inventors' and investors' fervor to be the first to market a writing machine and/or a mechanized system for setting type. The basics of word processing are even older.

The printing and publishing industry has always been quick to utilize new technology. Technology that many modern writers quickly learned to take for granted was made possible and affordable by an evolutionary series of printing and publishing innovations. The standard accoutrements for today's average writer might consist of a microprocessor, text manipulation program (word processor), CRT/LCD/ plasma screen, keyboard, and plain paper laser printer. These elements existed for many years in printing and publishing offices before they were commonplace in the writer's office. Technologically, the writer's electronic tools are not new, but vastly improved, and much cheaper. Although, for their size, they are faster and more powerful, their most significant feature is their price. Twenty years ago, a properly trained writer could compose on publishing/typesetting equipment with similar operating speeds and power, but instead of costing a few hundred dollars, the equipment costs exceeded $100,000.

Although writers tend to think of computer word processing as a relatively new technology, the concept of text manipulation is at least as old as Gutenberg's invention of movable type, and it has existed in one mechanical form or another since at least 1876 when the first mechanical typewriter was commercially produced. Despite the fact that word processors appear to be a relatively new technology to most users, word processing is not new to older printers and typographers who have used them since the early 1960s.

Machine word processing began in the late nineteenth century with the development of input keyboards and basic off-line storage techniques. Electronic writing began in 1948 when Eastman Kodak filed for a patent on devices that would display characters on a cathode ray tube (CRT) without having to physically create them first (Seybold and Seybold 18–3). Computer word processing began as early as 1954 when Bafour, Blanchard, and Raymond of France filed for a patent on a machine that would utilize a "special-purpose computer" to manipulate texts input onto punched tape (18–4). By the mid 1960s, development of scanning CRT typesetting devices (the parent of laser printer technology) was well underway. These devices held the information for text and character shapes in computer memory until directly scanned onto photosensitive film by a controlled CRT beam. For the first time, no physical matrix was needed to set type. Until the early 1970s, computerized word processors used mainframe or minicomputers. The use of a microcomputer for word processing in 1973 was one of the first commercial applications of the new technology (18–8).

Defining Writing Machines

The first step in understanding writing machine history is understanding what defines a writing machine. Out of the hundreds of methods humans have invented to record information, how are writing machines different from other writing tools such as the quill and paper? What do writing machines do that other writing tools cannot?

Whether for good or ill, many computer researchers assert that one of the computer's qualities as a writing machine is its ability to ease the task of text manipulation, in particular, editing and revising (i.e., McAllister and Louth; Daiute; Gerrard 96). Although the ability to ease the labor of revision and editing is an important aspect of writing machines, this expedience is secondary to, and dependent upon, the primary quality that all writing machines must possess: the ability to provide an unlimited supply of symbols for the writer to arrange. Despite the apparent complexity of today's computerized writing machines, this is still the primary function upon which all of the word processor's other functions rely.

Until the development and use of movable type in about 1450 by Johannes Gutenberg, in order to produce a readable text, writers had to create each individual character to form their texts (or dictate the information to someone who performed this task for them). Then movable type introduced the ability to create texts without the necessity of creating each character one after the other (the typefounder now performed that function), and like handwriting, movable type created a finished text that could be read albeit backward and upside down.

Incidental to freeing the writer from having to painstakingly form each character, writing machines generally allow the writer to more easily manipulate texts prior to its final appearance on paper. Direct entry systems such as the typewriter, while appearing to lack this ability, with the use of "cut and paste" techniques, still make revision easier than by hand.

The feature mechanical typewriters lack that most benefits text manipulation is the creation of some sort of off-line storage of text before its final output. The typewriter is a "direct entry" machine. Its output is created at the time the operator inputs the alpha/numeric characters. "Indirect entry" of text was developed with the invention of movable type, which created an off-line form of text storage in the form of galleys (relatively unformatted text being prepared for printing) and forms (formatted and paginated texts ready for printing). Galleys and forms could be manipulated by replacing or moving sections (or blocks) of type from one position to another, as opposed to completely rewriting or erasing and rewriting portions of the text. Correction of errors was also simplified because minor changes required minor alterations and did not necessitate resetting pages. Simply put, writing machines are different from pen, pencil, quill, burin, brush, chisel, paper, clay, wax tablet, and stone because they supply an essentially unlimited supply of letters and/or symbols to the writer without the necessity of the writer creating each individual character, and they generally reproduce texts in a mutable fashion for revision and editing before final output or transmission through electronic media.

Until the development of the typewriter, most writers seldom took advantage of the concept of writing from an unlimited supply of letters. After all, setting type from a typecase required availability of materials (the type) and technical skills (relief type must be read upside down and backward, a feat difficult for some people). However, it was a common practice for printers to compose texts at the typecase rather than compose it in manuscript. Writing by hand was redundant when the material had to be typeset anyway.

Writing machines not only ease the production of letters and words but more importantly for the writer, they ease the tasks of revision and editing. It is this ability to simplify revision and editing that leads writers away from the typewriter and to the word processor, not input speed or accuracy. Although typewriters seem clumsy at revision compared to word processors, they simplify revision compared to handwriting. Cut and paste, erasure and retyping are still more desirable than reproduction by hand, which requires more physical effort.

EFFICIENCY, ECONOMICS, AND WRITING MACHINE DEVELOPMENT

An innovation in technology is only useful when it is exploited. No persistent technology is ever attained for altruistic reasons. If there is no economic incentive to keep a technology extant, any technological innovation reaches a standstill and ceases to exist. Early experiments with movable type in China and Korea are cases in point.

Gutenberg and his contemporaries were not the first to invent movable type. Movable type was used as early as 1041–1049 AD. Douglas C. McMurtrie, typographer, book designer, and printing historian explains, "[t]he Chinese invention of separate types antedated the experiments of Gutenberg by more than four hundred years. The inventor was Pi Shêng, and his types were made of baked clay and not of metal" (95). Although the East experimented with movable type in many forms, including wood and metal as well as ceramics (96), the practice was eventually abandoned because it was too cumbersome to use with a writing system that incorporated thousands of symbols. While Western movable type requires about eighty to ninety bins in a typecase to hold all upper and lowercase letters as well as spacing material and punctuation, Chinese typecases need thousands of bins. This huge variety of necessary ideograms complicated typesetting, redistribution of type, punch cutting (the making of the matrices to cast the types), and type founding (the casting of the types). Though the altruistic incentive to preserve the art of typography in China and Korea was great, the art failed to survive because the economic incentive was hampered until more financially feasible methods were developed hundreds of years later. (The plethora of symbols in Oriental languages also complicated the development of typewriters and typesetting machines in those languages.)

Because of writing's importance to the growth of shared knowledge and the preservation of culture, people tend to ignore its dependence upon economic considerations for its preservation. This essential fact has been obscured perhaps most by those benefitting most from printing and writing technologies, from religions, to academics, to the printing industry itself. Religion uses writing to maintain traditions among the faithful, while educational institutions use writing to expand the ever growing tide of information, and many printers make their livelihoods by serving both. It is writing and printing that maintain the hoards of people who flock to these institutions for answers and guidance, thus perpetuating the institutions financially as well as in spirit. The art and craft of printing is an example of how writing's commercial success has been glossed over for altruistic reasons. In the past, printing was continually touted by writers and philosophers as a high point in humanity's achievements: "The second part of the history of the world and the arts begins with the invention of printing" (Zapf 20, 109).

> The printer is the friend of intelligence, of thought; he is the friend of liberty, of freedom, of law; indeed, the printer is the friend of every man who is the friend of order—the friend of every man who can read! Of all the inventions, of all the discoveries in science or art, of all the great results in the wonderful progress of mechanical energy and skill, the printer is the only product of civilisation necessary to the existence of free man. (Charles Dickens qtd. in Zapf 110)

High praise indeed. This pedestal upon which printing is placed tends to obscure the fact that printing, like all developing technologies, was primarily pursued for economic reasons and later adapted to altruistic uses. This is also true for even the most ancient developments of writing technology. Albertine Gaur, Deputy Director of Oriental Collections at the British Library writes in *A History of Writing*:

> Most codified forms of writing using (a varying amount of) phonetic elements developed in capitalistically-orientated societies with a primitive technology: between 4000–3000 BC in

> the Fertile Crescent, about 2000 BC in the Far East (the very
> latest discoveries may add another millennium to this date),
> and perhaps around 1000 BC in Central America. Indeed
> many of the early documents written in those scripts relate
> to property. In Mesopotamia, Egypt and the ancient Aegean
> we come across lists of goods sold, transferred or received, let-
> ters, contracts, administrative accounts and records. [. . .] Only
> gradually, and in many cases after a good deal of controversy,
> does the new codified form of writing replace oral traditions in
> the field of religious and secular literature. (17)

Because writing originally preserved and expedited wealth and power,
because wealth and power crave increase, writing evolved to keep up
with the demand, becoming more efficient, more accurate, and more
easily stored and transported. It was not until after writing technology
and techniques were developed that the arts and philosophy utilized
them. Altruistic endeavors are the users of technology, not the motiva-
tors of technology.

When financial, religious, or political considerations demanded more copies, writing technology naturally accommodated, from
improved writing surfaces to improved writing instruments. In the
development of writing technology, the need always precedes the development, thus motivating fertile minds to fill the vacuum. This is
not to imply that those at the forefront of innovation have merely financial or political gain in mind, but after they achieve their contribution, it is gain that decides whether or not the innovation succeeds or
fails.

The success of writing machines since the invention of movable
type requires improvements in the speed or convenience of input and/
or text manipulation to be successful. An innovation succeeds only if
it improves one or both of these features, and only then is it incorporated into a new generation of writing machines. Contrary to common
belief, Gutenberg's significance to the world of printing was not the
printing press. Although the printing press sped up the production
of duplicating books, it was movable type that sped up the process of
copying manuscripts for printing. Movable type required a typesetter to copy the manuscript only once. All other copies were produced
from the typeset master. Until that time, if one wanted to duplicate a
text through printing, the text had to be hand cut in either wood or
metal. Together, movable type and the screw press were more conve-

nient and less expensive than armies of scribes. By the same token, the Linotype, Monotype, and Ludlow typesetting machines were more convenient and less expensive than armies of hand compositors.

Although Gutenberg was probably the first to apply a screw to a printing press, relief printing existed long before movable type. As previously stated, Gutenberg's primary contribution to printing history was a practical method to make and use movable type. Historian and past Library of Congress librarian Daniel J. Boorstin emphasizes this fact when he writes:

> His crucial invention was actually not so much a new way of "printing" as a new way of multiplying the metal type for individual letters. [. . .] Gutenberg's crucial invention was his specially designed mold for casting precisely similar pieces of type quickly and in large numbers. This was a machine tool—a tool for making the machines (i.e., the type) that did the printing. (510–511)

Although the printing of texts from a single carved form (generally wood) was a common practice in some Asian countries, the idea never gained popularity in Europe. It was left to the inventor of moveable type to make mass production of identical texts feasible and practical in the West.

Gutenberg's motivations for his innovations were, in large part, economic. Certainly he understood the financial possibilities, for he spent a great deal of time attempting to amass funds from investors, and later, even more time involved in litigations against him (510–513). In the West, printing from movable type was an efficient and cost effective way to reproduce information at a time when a knowledge explosion was taking place during the Renaissance, and Gutenberg's timing was perfect to satisfy an information-hungry world.

MOVABLE TYPE AND THE BASICS OF ALL WRITING MACHINES

The invention of movable type in the West was more than an advance in the duplication of texts; it was also the beginning of mechanical writing. Four hundred and twenty years after Gutenberg's invention Mark Twain remarked in a letter to his brother Orion Clemens that:

> WORKING THE TYPE-WRITER REMINDS ME OF OLD
> ROBERT BUCHANAN, WHO, YOU REMEMBER, USED TO
> SET UP ARTICLES AT THE CASE WITHOUT PREVIOUSLY
> PUTTING THEM IN THE FORM OF MANUSCRIPT. I WAS
> LOST IN ADMIRATION OF SUCH MARVELOUS INTEL-
> LECTUAL CAPACITY. (Bliven 61; Romano 12)

From the time of the English printer, William Caxton, to Mark
Twain's printing and typesetting mentor, Robert Buchanan, it was
not uncommon for printers to serve as authors, editors, and transla-
tors. Just like "old Robert Buchanan" many of them circumvented the
act of shaping the letters by pen and composed the text at the typecase instead, especially when making small changes to texts already
typeset. This method of composition easily carried over to typesetting
machines. This circumvention of handwritten copy is the basis of all
writing machines, and the concept of writing without pen began with
the invention of movable type.

The process used to produce a printing matrix from handset type
for duplication by letterpress is conceptually the same as the basic process used by word processors. The recorded material for the computer
differs in that it is held electronically until recalled to be altered or output, whereas the letterpress form is physical. Both forms exist and can
be altered and reproduced without the use of pen or paper.

The actual process of composing the text from a typecase is
slower than by computer, but the reason for this has nothing to do
with the computer processor and everything to do with the method
of input—fingers striking keys on a keyboard as opposed to fingers
grasping and arranging letters from a case. The computer improves
processing speeds and can quickly manipulate texts and react to texts
in various ways according to the program running, whereas in manual typesetting, each function must be performed one-at-a-time with
care and concentration of the typographer during the process. In both
cases, the data must be input before manipulation of the data can be
achieved. Both handsetting type and keyboarding do not require the
individual shaping of each letter, and they yield a form that exists prior
to impression, and a form that can be altered and reproduced without
re-inputting the entire text.

Along with the concept of an unlimited supply of letters, movable
type also introduced a new and significant aspect of machine writing (and word processing): off-line storage that can be edited without

marring the final copy. With movable type, once a text is typeset, if errors are found or changes need to be made, it is a matter of resetting one portion of the text and correcting the error before printing. After printing, the type can be redistributed into cases and used again, or it can be saved for later reprints and revisions.

The concepts of writing from an inexhaustible supply of letters and auxiliary storage were known to all printers, and although many non-printing writers were familiar with the basics of printing, because of the costs, complexity, and skills required to compose with type, few authors could use that system for writing. So, the methods of the writer remained essentially the same from the invention of the quill pen until the invention of the first commercially successful typewriter.

EVOLUTION OF THE PRINTING PRESS AND TYPESETTING

The method of setting type changed little from 1450 until the beginning of the nineteenth century. In contrast, the end of the eighteenth century saw a major step forward in printing press construction due to advances made in the techniques of casting metal, "and in the rise of a class of mechanics, the forerunners of the engineers, who were to transform the nineteenth-century industrial scene" (Moran 49). One of the most significant advances was the development of a class of letterpresses that did not require the paper to be dampened before printing. (Like intaglio presses, screw presses required the paper be dampened so the ink would better adhere to the sheet.) Not having to wet the sheet sped up production speeds by a huge margin. Other machine advances, including the web-fed printing press and inexpensive paper (made from tree pulp instead of more expensive animal organs or fabric fibers), revolutionized printing production by reducing the costs of materials and increasing production speeds even more.

Although the appearance and operation of printing presses began to change drastically in the early nineteenth century, there were few, if any, appreciable changes in the methods used to set the type for printing or to write the manuscripts that would eventually be typeset and printed. Although the demand for typesetting increased because of the increase in periodicals, newspapers, and the variety of books printed, publishing houses could only respond by hiring ever larger armies of typographers to get the job done. The increase in published material also created a need to speed up the writing process itself.

Parallel Development of the
Typewriter and Typesetter

As the demand for publishing increased, so did the demand for texts to be typeset and published. As publishing houses printed a larger variety of texts, it became clear that whoever automated typesetting would not only make a major contribution to the dissemination of texts but stood to make a great deal of money as well.

The situation for the typewriter was similar:

> [T]he pen was annoyingly slow. An expert penman, trying his best, might be able to write at a rate of thirty words per minute, but most writers were something less than expert. The tedium was bad enough in itself, but after 1840, when Samuel F. B. Morse patented his electric telegraph, it seemed worse. In short order a whole generation of telegraphers had appeared who could understand code a lot faster than they could write it down. Shorthand stenographers were in a similar fix. They could take their notes as quickly as a man could speak, and yet they couldn't transcribe faster than at a snail's pace. (Bliven 35)

Not to mention that handwriting was hard to read, and showed no signs of getting better (35).

It became clear that whoever found a way to alleviate the drudgery of writing would benefit society and their own pocketbook every bit as much as the developer of an automated typesetting machine. Early evidence of the need for a writing machine emphasized the commercial promise of such a machine and was recorded in 1647 when Charles I granted a patent to William Petty for a machine which "might be learnt in an hour's time, and of great advantage to lawyers, scriveners, merchants, scholars, registrars, clerks, etcetera; it saving the labour of examination, discovering or preventing falsification, and performing the business of writing—as with ease and speed—so with privacy" (Beeching 3). Petty's machine appears to be a sort of pantograph machine for writing with two pens at once (3). It shows an early interest in reducing the labor of writing, and especially copying. It also shows that the primary desire to develop the machine stemmed from commercial reasons and not altruistic ones. Less than sixty years later the first documented typewriter was patented: "A prominent English engineer, Henry Mill, was the first, as far as anybody knows, to think up the basic idea of a typewriter. Queen Anne granted him a Royall Letters Patent on January 7, 1714. [. . .] Mill presumably made a model" (Bliven 24).

Despite these early attempts at a writing machine, the technique of writing did not change. Although patents had been granted for a variety of writing and copying machines, it was not until 1873 that Christopher Latham Sholes and his backers demonstrated to Philo Remington, president of a family business making firearms, sewing machines, and farm machinery, what proved to be the first typewriter that could be commercially-produced successfully.

Progress in the development of typesetting machines began considerably later than the typewriter. Although the printing press was continually modified over the five hundred years following Gutenberg, the method of setting type remained the same. A punch cutter had to punch the matrices for the type, a founder had to make the type, and a compositor had to hand-set the type from cases. Although handsetting type and printing by letterpress was faster than a scribe, the development of commerce, made possible in large part by mass-produced texts, required faster and faster production times. This could only be accomplished by armies of typographers and more foundries producing type. The problem was finally resolved when Ottmar Mergenthaler unveiled the first commercially viable typesetting machine—the Linotype—on July 3, 1886 in the composing room of *The Tribune* in New York City (Romano 63). The Linotype became the first commercially-produced and used typesetting machine, and it was commonplace in print shops into the 1950s and 1960s.

As with Sholes's "Type-Writer," Mergenthaler's Linotype was not so much a new invention as a successful combination of ideas generated by a mechanical evolution that was greatly accelerated during the latter part of the nineteenth century. Mergenthaler's was one of many attempts to mechanize the otherwise meticulous task of setting type. One of these attempts, the Paige Compositor designed by inventor James W. Paige, eventually drove Mark Twain to the lecture circuit to recover his investment losses (82). During that machine's development, Twain wrote to friend and author William D. Howells in 1889 that he had spent "more than $3,000 a month on it for 44 consecutive months" (Twain and Howells 288). Twain, as an experienced printer and typesetter, as well as successful published author, was willing to spend over $132,000 on the machine because he recognized its great commercial potential, not only for the publishing business but for turning his considerable investment into a considerable profit. Unfortunately for Twain, the Paige Compositor was never produced commercially.

Of all the attempts at mechanical typesetting during the last two decades of the nineteenth century, two machines were produced well into the twentieth, Mergenthaler's Linotype and Tolbert Lanston's Monotype. The Linotype casts lines of type from individual recirculating brass matrices (mats) and recirculating wedges (space bands). When the operator depresses a key on the machine's keyboard, a single mat drops from the magazine onto a belt that transports it to the position where it is aligned with the other characters to create a single line of type. The wedge-shaped space bands are pushed up, spreading the mats to justify the type to the proper line measure. When the line is justified to the operator's satisfaction, a lever is pulled and the justified line is transferred to the casting mechanism. After the line has been cast, the space bands are returned for reuse, and each mat is returned to its individual tube, or "channel," in the magazine via an elevating mechanism and the transfer bar. From the transfer bar, the mats are sorted and stored in a large magazine that contains many channels for this purpose. Each mat has a unique "key" cut into it. A rotating distribution bar moves the mats along the top of the magazine. When a mat encounters the cut in the distribution bar that matches its key, it drops into its proper channel ready for reuse.

The Monotype casts lines of type from hot metal as well, but, as its name implies, it casts each character individually. The resulting line of type looks very much like a compositor had set the line from foundry type by hand. The Monotype system consists of two machines, the keyboard and the casting mechanism. The operator depresses a key, the keyboard punches the code for the key on a punched tape. The power for the tape puncher is provided by compressed air. As the operator inputs the material, a rotating scale mounted on the keyboard indicates how much space is left on the line being set. By observing the scale, the operator can tell when to end a line and how much extra space is needed between each letter to justify the text. This information is punched on the tape as well. After completion of the inputting process, the tape is placed in the separate casting mechanism that uses compressed air to read the characters from the punched tape, much like a player piano. The matrices for the type are punched on a square, brass matrix that is positioned by the machine over the caster. The caster, which changes widths to accommodate the character matrix above it, casts each type individually, including word spaces, until the line is completed. The completed line is removed to a holding area, and the caster begins the next line until the tape runs out.

These are very simple descriptions of extremely complex mechanical devices utilizing hundreds of precision moving parts and weighing hundreds of pounds. So complex, yet reliable was the Linotype that "Thomas Alva Edison referred to the Linotype as the 'Eighth Wonder of the World'" (Romano 104). Although much more temperamental than the Linotype, the Monotype produces an even finer quality of type and has cast type for many of academia's finest volumes in such publishing houses as the Oxford University Press and the University of California Press.

At this juncture it is important to note that typecasting machine operators and hand compositors make virtually all typographic decisions, including line endings, hyphenation, page breaks, pagination, etc., and the type is set one line at a time. The decision making that is required by typography is so complex that it would not be until the 1950s that machines could be developed that could reliably take over most of these functions.

Two Early Writing Machine Innovations

The industrial revolution began a period of rapid technological development, motivated by profit, that continues today. With the development of various models and styles of typewriters and typesetting machines, the groundwork for all writing machines was completed during this century and the first machines were produced by its conclusion. Many of the basic processes modern writing machines use were developed at that time including auxiliary storage devices and keyboards to input data. Although the invention of the first digital computer did not occur until the late 1930s (Shelly and Cashman 2.2), two of the primary means by which computers stored information until the release of the floppy disk in the early 1970s were being used by the last decade of the nineteenth century: the punched card and punched tape. During the nineteenth century the methods the West used to print, set type, and write changed forever because of modern technology.

THE DEVELOPMENT OF THE KEYBOARD

Neither Mergenthaler's Linotype machine nor Sholes's "Type-Writer" were original ideas. They were successful inventions utilizing a variety of inventions from a variety of inventors from a variety of countries. They were developed to fulfill the need to write and reproduce writing more quickly—a motivation that preceded their production by at least one hundred years and continues to the present day.

The success of typewriters and typesetting machines lay, in part, with how information was input. They were machines of convenience and efficiency, so the development of an efficient inputting system that did not require too much time to learn, or too much time and energy to operate, was important to their intended function. Because the purpose of both the typewriter and the mechanical typesetter was to be able to perform their respective tasks considerably faster than by traditional methods, the operators had to be able to input information more quickly than had been done by hand. In order to achieve this, inventors took a hint from the musical keyboard:

> When early producers of typewriters first directed their thoughts to a keyboard, they were obsessed with the arrangement of the piano keyboard. [. . .] People, after all, had been playing pianos for 200 years and remember, the basic principles of the piano have changed very little, and the keyboard remains the same today. It is universally understood in any country throughout the world. Given these simple facts, perhaps it is understandable that those who were striving to make a Writing Machine could not see beyond this musical instrument and its general layout. (Beeching 39)

Although some of the mechanics of the musical keyboard could be applied to writing machines, the layout proved to be impractical, leaving inventors to devise their own: "Early machines showed a vast variety of keyboard arrangements. Some were circular, others had three to eight or ten rows of keys; and some had no shift keys whilst others had one or two" (39). Out of this myriad of keyboards, one keyboard became the standard for most western countries. The keyboard we are most familiar with is referred to as the "QWERTY" for the first six letters at the top left of the keyboard. Despite its ubiquitous persistence, Sholes, the inventor of the QWERTY keyboard, did not design it with ergonomics in mind. The concepts of touch typing, memorizing the keyboard, or typing without looking at the keys were not motivations for QWERTY's inventor. In fact, it was left to the operators of the device, not Sholes, to devise touch typing. Sholes was interested in producing a successful writing machine, not advanced typing techniques.

The QWERTY keyboard was an innovation intended to overcome mechanical obstacles Sholes was facing. Sholes originally designed his keyboard with four rows of keys arranged alphabetically, and it only typed uppercase letters. This arrangement proved troublesome. As operators typed, they had a tendency to jam the machine, because they could type faster than the machine could return the typebars to their resting positions. Sholes's solution was a different arrangement of letters:

> [Sholes] found that the "ABC" arrangement [of his earlier keyboard] caused his [. . .] machine to jam when any speed was reached and, realizing the insurmountable technical problems arising from this, which had exhausted both his skill and patience, he cast around for other means of resolving his dilemma. He sought the advice of his brother-in-law who was a schoolmaster and mathematician, and asked him to re-arrange the keyboard so that, on most occasions, the bars would come up from opposite directions and would not clash together and jam the machine.
>
> After many calculations and experiments, [Sholes] established the existing keyboard on which the first six letters are Q W E R T Y, and departed from all previous alphabetical arrangements. [He] then proceeded to sell this "QWERTY" arrangement of the keyboard. It was probably one of the biggest confidence tricks of all time—namely the idea that this arrangement of the keyboard was scientific and added speed and efficiency. This, of course, was true of his particular machine, but the idea that the so-called 'scientific arrangement' of the keys was designed to give the minimum movement of the hands was, in fact, completely false! To write almost any

> word in the English language, a maximum distance has to be
> covered by the fingers. (39–40)

The keyboard used for virtually all English language computer keyboards is not based upon efficiency for the operator, but efficiency for a mechanical device designed over one hundred years ago.

The QWERTY keyboard became the English language standard as the result of a contest between two expert typists. In 1888, Frank E. McGurrin, "stenographer for the Federal Court in Salt Lake City and a first class typist" (40) issued an open challenge to test his keyboarding prowess. McGurrin taught himself the touch technique using a Remington Model No. 1, very similar to Sholes's original machine. The Model No. 1 had four rows of eleven keys each and was the same basic keyboard layout that is in use today. The Model No. 1 typed only uppercase letters. Because McGurrin memorized the keyboard, he did not need to move his eyes from the copy as he typed.

During the time of McGurrin's challenge "hunt and peck" schools of typing outnumbered those that advocated ten-finger typing and the memorization of the keyboard. At the time, there were many keyboard arrangements on the market. An adherent of one of these alternate keyboard designs, Louis Taub, convinced he was the world's fastest typist, accepted McGurrin's challenge. Taub used a typewriter made by the Caligraph company. The Caligraph machine had six rows of keys with no shift mechanism. It typed both lower and uppercase letters with one key for each. With six rows of twelve keys each, and the keyboard had seventy-two keys compared to Remington's forty-four.

> The race was to be in two parts: forty-five minutes of direct
> dictation and forty-five minutes of copying from an unfamil-
> iar script, and the man with the larger combined total number
> of words would win. The stake was $500. [. . .] [McGurrin]
> won both separate events in addition to the aggregate. Typists
> all over the country noticed an extraordinary feature of his
> triumph. He had actually gone faster working from copy than
> when he had taken dictation. (Bliven 114–115)

Along with showing the world the expediency of touch typing, McGurrin inadvertently sold the keyboard he was using—the same Remington keyboard modified by Sholes's brother-in-law. Because of the contest's worldwide publicity, most manufacturers began to modify their machines to accept the QWERTY layout. Those that did not lost any competitive edge in typewriter sales and production.

Although the QWERTY keyboard became the American standard for typewriters, there were still individuals who felt there were other designs that could improve operator speed and accuracy. It was not until 1905 that the QWERTY was firmly established as the norm for English language typewriters:

> In 1905 a large international meeting was called to establish a standard keyboard once and for all. At that time various keyboards—certainly more efficient than the one devised by Sholes and used today—were put forward as alternatives. The battle raged backwards and forwards. Nobody could agree on what a new keyboard should be, but the biggest opposition came from *teachers of typing* as it still does today. They wanted things to remain as they were, and they are still reluctant to change their methods and learn all over again. (Beeching 41)

It is interesting to note that teachers are as guilty as inventors for the clumsy keyboard we use today.

During the years between 1895 and 1931 there were many improvements in the development of the typewriter and typewriting techniques. In 1895 the top speed of an efficient typist was in the neighborhood of one hundred words per minute (wpm). Contests held in New York and Toronto in 1888 yielded speeds of 95.2 to 98.7 wpm (Bliven 116–118). Through improved technique and machines, speeds increased dramatically over the next thirty years. In 1923 Albert Tangora "did 147 net actual words per minute on his Underwood Model 5" (130). Tangora's feat was produced on a manual typewriter first produced in 1915 (Beeching 214–215).

Although the QWERTY became the standard for offices and business, it was not the standard for printing and publishing. Typecasting keyboards differed from typewriter keyboards for several reasons. First, the function of a typesetting machine was considerably different from the function of a typewriter, as were their mechanical requirements (a typewriter might weigh a few pounds; a Linotype machine weighs over one thousand pounds). In addition, typesetters need a host of characters not utilized in office and personal correspondence, including fractions, ligatures, diphthongs, and specialized punctuation, including a variety of long dashes, fixed spaces, and open and closed single and double quotation marks.

The Linotype keyboard was a triple keyboard with six horizontal rows of fifteen keys each. The lowercase letters were located on the left side, figures and punctuation in the middle, and uppercase letters on the right. One keyboarding technique encouraged by manufacturers required the left hand operate the first two rows of the keyboard, and the right hand roamed the rest of the keyboard for the other characters. This meant that approximately one-fourth of the keyboard was handled by the left hand, leaving the remaining three-fourths to be handled by the right hand (Barbour). As with the typewriter, Linotype operators were encouraged to use touch systems to keep their eyes free to observe the copy and the rest of the machine (Intertype Corporation 440). Average typesetting speeds on the Linotype machine ran approximately twenty to thirty words per minute. Mark Barbour, curator of the International Printing Museum in Buena Park, California, explained in a telephone interview that "Forty words per minute would be a very good speed of a good operator per minute. I think if you want to talk about the average operator you are talking about half to two thirds for a good operator."

Part of the reason for the discrepancy in speed between typewriter operators and typesetting machine operators was the layout of the keyboards. The much larger typesetting machine keyboards did not allow many common words to be input from a "home" position like the typewriter, but required constant "roaming" of the keyboard by both hands. Typesetting machine operators also had more typographic concerns such as justification and the addition of alternate characters not available on the keyboard.

Several keyboard-style typecasting machines were developed after the Linotype. The Intertype was, for all intents and purposes, identical to the Linotype. The Monotype, previously discussed, had a different keyboard. Keyboard operations of the various typecasting machines varied from manufacturer to manufacturer. Barbour explained there were specific schools set up for teaching operators, mostly by the manufacturers, and keyboarding techniques varied. Also, like the typewriter, there were annual trade competitions to test the speed and accuracy of operators. These contests, still held today, never received the level of international attention paid to typewriter speed contests.

As with the typewriter, virtually all successful typesetting machines utilized a keyboard for input except the Ludlow machine, first marketed in 1911 by the Ludlow Typograph Company (Seybold and Seybold 18–3). The Ludlow was intended to set larger display type, and type matrices were assembled on a composing stick, similar to handset type, prior to casting. Despite the success of machines like the Linotype and the Monotype, because of advancing technology, particularly the teletype machine and the computer, printing and publishing eventually adopted the QWERTY as its standard keyboard.

The fact that the QWERTY keyboard arrangement dominates computer as well as typewriter keyboards is not a testament to any ergonomic thought on Christopher Latham Sholes's part, but to the difficulty people encounter when first learning to type and their refusal to change their operating habits for more efficient methods. This difficulty is caused by several aspects of the keyboard: first, touch typing requires very complex and rapid movements of all ten fingers in conjunction with mental activities that vary with the type of work being performed, from transcription to taking dictation to generative typing. Second, the experience of learning to type is fraught with so much work and frustration that the thought of learning to use another keyboard layout, whether more efficient or not, is repulsive to most typists. So, we are faced with a paradox: for the sake of efficiency, learning even the clumsy QWERTY keyboard is worth the effort, yet few desire to apply the limited effort needed to gain the considerable advantages learning an even more efficient keyboard arrangement offers.

Despite its clumsiness, the QWERTY keyboard represented a faster method of performing writing tasks. Besides being faster, it was reasonably accurate, and its various output devices (typewriters, typesetters, teletype machines, etc.) provided universally legible copy. Both typewriters and typesetters needed it if they were going to achieve their objective of speeding up the composing and printing processes. Although the mechanics (and electronics) of the keyboard have been constantly improved, no method of machine input has been devised to replace it.

It is unlikely current research into alternate methods of inputting data into computers will soon replace the keyboard. Although computer research and development is working on handwriting recognition systems, it is unlikely they will be much more than a novelty for those with good keyboarding skills. These devices require writing by hand, the very process typewriters were developed to replace in most situations. Voice recognition systems have a great deal of promise for those not wishing to type, but speech recognition systems, while constantly improving, need a great deal more improvement before they replace the speed, efficiency, and accuracy of competent keyboardists.

As is evidenced by the factors contributing to the design of the QWERTY keyboard, the efficiency of their writing machines was the inventors' sole priority. Their objective was to develop machines that would speed up the composition, transcription, and dictation processes—machines that would sell well—and this they did. As is the case with many machines, the development of efficient operating techniques was left to be puzzled out later by operators and manufacturers.

WORKS CITED

Barbour, Mark. Telephone interview. 28 June 1994.

Beeching, Wilfred A. *Century of the Typewriter*. New York: St. Martin's Press, 1974. Print.

Bliven, Bruce, Jr. *The Wonderful Writing Machine*. New York: Random House, 1954. Print.

Boorstin, Daniel J. *The Discoverers*. New York: Random House, 1983. Print.

Daiute, Colette. *Writing and Computers*. Reading, MA: Addison-Wesley Publishing Company, Inc., 1985. Print.

Gaur, Albertine. *A History of Writing*. New York: Cross River Press, 1992. Print.

Gerrard, Lisa. "Computers and Basic Writers: A Critical View." *Critical Perspectives on Computers and Composition Instruction*. Ed. Gail E. Hawisher and Cynthia L. Selfe. New York: Teachers College Press, 1989. 94–108. Print.

Intertype Corporation. *The Intertype: A Book of Instruction for its Operation and General Maintenance*. Brooklyn, NY: Intertype Corp., 1943. Print

McAllister, Carole, and Richard Louth. "The Effect of Word Processing on the Quality of Basic Writers' Revisions." *Research in the Teaching of English* 22 (1988): 417–427. Print.

McMurtrie, Douglas C. *The Book: The Story of Printing & Bookmaking*. New York: Dorset Press, 1989. Print.

Moran, James. *Printing Presses: History and Development from the Fifteenth Century to Modern Times*. Berkeley: U of California P, 1978. Print.

Romano, Frank J. *Machine Writing and Typesetting: The Story of Sholes and Mergenthaler and the Invention of the Typewriter and the Linotype*. Salem, NH: GAMA, 1986. Print.

Seybold, John W., and Jonathan Seybold. "Typesetting and Pre-Press Technology: A Chronology from 1822 to 1984." *The Seybold Report* 13.18 (1984): 18.3–18.23. Print.

Shelly, Gary B., and Thomas J. Cashman. *Introduction to Computers and Data Processing.* Brea, CA: Anaheim Publishing, 1980. Print.

Twain, Mark and William D. Howells. *Selected Mark Twain-Howells Letters: 1872–1910.* Ed. Frederick Anderson, William M. Gibson, and Henry Nash Smith. New York: Atheneum, 1967. Print.

Zapf, Hermann. *Manuale Typographicum.* Cambridge, MA: MIT Press, 1970. Print.

4 "The Next Takes the Machine": Typewriter Technology and the Transformation of Teaching

Shawn Fullmer

> *When the first pupil has written his sentences, the next takes the machine, writes his, and then the next, and so on, till the entire class has completed the task.*
>
> —William A. Mowry

William A. Mowry's words, published in 1891, reveal many American educators' optimistic expectations about the new writing technology known as the typewriter. Within decades after commercial manufacturing of the typewriter began in 1873, educators at all levels, elementary, secondary, and college, were integrating the typewriter into the classroom. This integration reflected the eventual and commonplace use of the typewriter in public, private, and business sectors. According to educator Frank H. Palmer in the June, 1892 edition of *Education,* "over two hundred thousand typewriting machines of all makes have been put upon the market in the past ten years [. . .] [and] typewriters have been introduced into over two hundred schools in New England alone, mostly within the past year" (628). However, unlike the private sector's and secondary and college teachers' interests in the typewriter as a vocational instrument, elementary educators hoped the typewriter would offer students "the possibility of facilitating their mastery" of language subjects (Haefner 17). In the elementary schools, that mastery meant, as Frasier points out across his foreword, the promotion of fundamental subjects, , such as reading, composition, and even spelling. For many educators, the typewriter embodied both a means and a method for improving learning and teaching. A method of teaching characterized by a "form-al" approach to writing instruction—with emphasis being on the form of letters, the form of paragraphs and sentences, and the form of accepted styles and models.

While investigations about the actual use of the typewriter in educational settings have been conducted, little analysis and inquiry into the *rhetoric* of the typewriter has been done. To illustrate the importance of the typewriter in the history and future of pedagogy, I examine the rhetoric of the typewriter in elementary educational settings by surveying the history of the typewriter, analyzing rhetoric of the typewriter based on the Toulmin scheme, and drawing connections between form-al pedagogy and rhetoric of the typewriter.

RHETORIC OF THE TYPEWRITER

In analyzing rhetoric of the typewriter, I draw upon Stephen Toulmin's description of argumentative structures, which "is remarkable for its clarity, flexibility, and reasonableness" (Bizzell and Herzberg 1104). Toulmin, in *The Uses of Argument*, explains how an argument can be viewed as a movement from data to a claim (a conclusion) by means of a warrant ("general, hypothetical statements," which act as "bridges" between the data and claim [98]). Toulmin further refines the argumentative structure by describing backing of the warrant and qualifiers and rebuttals.

Following Toulmin's scheme, I provide data, illustrate the claim (conclusion) made by educators, show the educators' warrants and backing for their claim, and consider qualifiers and rebuttals. Data for my rhetorical analysis of educators' claims concerning the typewriter consists of research and opinions about the typewriter from the 1860s to the 1980s. The majority of this data comes from academic journals—*Education, The Psychological Bulletin, Elementary School Journal*—and the "Elementary School Typewriter Investigation," comprised of *An Experimental Study of the Educational Influences of the Typewriter on the Elementary School Classroom* and *The Typewriter in the Primary and Intermediate Grades: A Basic Educational Instrument for Younger Children*. Collectively, the educators in all of these texts claim the typewriter should be introduced and/or maintained in the elementary school classroom as an instrument for promoting the fundamental school subjects, such as reading, spelling, and composition.

Documented expectations and claims about the use of the typewriter in school classrooms are evident as early as 1887. General Thomas J. Morgan, Commissioner of Indian Affairs, observes in *Education* that:

> The habits of care, neatness, accuracy, and skill necessary to a successful manipulation of the typewriter enter into the intellectual make-up of the pupil, and reappear in whatever he may undertake to do. One of the most obvious advantages is a more perfect mastery of the English language. If he uses the typewriter, the student must give attention not only to spelling, capitalizing, punctuating, sentence-making, and paragraphing, but also to the weightier matters—thought and style. Poverty of idea and infelicities of style are more apparent on a printed page than when disguised in poor chirography or veneered with elegant penmanship. (qtd. in Mowry)

Although Morgan has loftier aspirations for the typewriter—alluding, with the word "thought," to knowledge making and identity shaping by and of students—he nevertheless echoes form-alist approaches to "mastery of the English language" by considering "style" and "spelling, capitalizing, punctuating, sentence-making, and paragraphing." It is clear Morgan believes the typewriter should, and will, be used in the classroom to promote "fundamental school subjects." Morgan intimates that the typewriter, through standardized printing of letters and characters, will enable form-alist educators to more accurately assess student performance.

During the 1890s and early 1900s, a few educators considered and promoted the typewriter's evaluative merits (Mowry 1891; Palmer 1892; Waldo 1902) and some research was done into the performance of adults using the typewriter (Swift 1904; Swift and Schuyler 1907). Observing a gap, Ralph S. Rowland noted that educators needed to conduct more empirical research about the typewriter in elementary classrooms, and that educators should address three "fundamental considerations" about the typewriter:

(1) Is there a universal need for skill in typewriting which would justify giving instruction in the subject in the elementary school the purpose of which is partly 'to develop that practical efficiency in activities shared by all in daily work and intercourse'? (2) Can pupils of elementary-school age learn to typewrite well, or can this instruction be given more effectively at an older age? (3) Is it possible that extended practice in typewriting might result in physiological harm to the pupils because of the muscular co-ordinations involved? (534–535)

In "An Experiment in Teaching Touch Typewriting to Pupils in the Fifth and Sixth Grades" (1930), Rowland seeks to illuminate the second question. During the 1928–1929 semester, Rowland studied the process by which a group of fifth and sixth grade pupils, in Lincoln, Nebraska, learned touch typing. He examined nineteen children for a period of fifteen weeks. Rowland was interested in "throw[ing] some light on [. . .] the question as to how well pupils in the elementary school can learn typewriting" (535). Rowland notes "the pupils were tested each week from the seventh to the fifteenth week [for] speed and accuracy combined" (535). He concludes that fifth and sixth grade children learned to type at least as well, if not better, than junior high school students. More interesting than Rowland's conclusion, however, is the rhetoric he uses to describe the typewriter.

> From the advent of typewriting into the schools up to the present time, the subject has been treated distinctly as a commercial subject and has been offered in high school and college to those who are preparing for office work. Recently typewriting has been introduced into many of the junior high schools in the country, but even there it is given chiefly as an exploratory, or prevocational course. We are just beginning to realize that typewriting may have great value for persons other than stenographers, that the rank and file of humanity may profit immensely from the ability to use a machine for easy, rapid, and legible writing. Typewriting is coming to be recognized as one of the more practical subjects taught in the schools. (533)

Rowland promotes educators' claims that the typewriter should be used in the elementary school classroom because it offers the possibility for students to produce legible, well-formed writing. Similar to

Morgan, Rowland envisions the impact the typewriter will have on teaching writing in the future.

Recognizing the need to address considerations similar to those posed by Rowland, the "Elementary School Typewriter Investigation" (1929 to 1931) was formed with the purpose of conducting a longitudinal and focused inquiry into the benefits and drawbacks of using the typewriter as an educational instrument for elementary students. Based upon empirical research, in the form of control group case studies, the "Elementary School Typewriter Investigation" planned to examine and possibly support claims that the typewriter:

> [H]as values, over and above its possible contribution to the pupils' later need of rapid writing. It must be clearly demonstrated that with the help of the machine, elementary school children are able to engage in stimulating sorts of activities which are either impossible or very difficult by means of other forms of expression, such as handwriting. The concrete evidence [. . .] [and] the illustrative materials shown there indicate that the machine provides the child with a valuable additional means of expression. (Haefner 36)

Concerned about the impact of the typewriter on pedagogy (and ironically and perhaps suspiciously funded and supplied by the four principle typewriter manufacturers) Ben D. Wood and Frank N. Freeman began studying the use of the typewriter in elementary schools in 1929. The study included 419 teachers and 14,949 students from fifty-one public and private schools. Wood and Freeman, collaborating with elementary school teachers and administrators, painstakingly collected questionnaires and artifacts (student samples, classroom photographs, assignments), and conducted interviews with administrators, teachers, and students. Their work provides lucid and detailed portraits and accounts of 1930s pedagogical methods synthesized with typewriter technology.

Wood and Freeman forward the claim that the typewriter should be introduced and/or maintained in the elementary school classroom as an instrument for promoting the fundamental school subjects most clearly and succinctly in the summary of *An Experimental Study of the Educational Influences of the Typewriter in the Elementary School Classroom.* They conclude:

(1) that it is feasible to use the typewriter in the conduct of the ordinary work in the elementary school, (2) that the use of the typewriter in the informal fashion in which it was employed in this study produces an average typing speed approximately equal to the average handwriting rate in each grade, and also yields a very considerable degree of typing accuracy at the end of one year's use, (3) that the use of the typewriter stimulates elementary school pupils to produce more written material than they would otherwise produce, (4) that the classroom typewriter, as used in this experiment, entails no loss in handwriting quality or handwriting rate, (5) that it very probably raises in some measure the level of achievement in some of the fundamental school subjects, without observable loss in any subject, and finally (6) that the teachers regard the typewriter as a valuable educational instrument and approve its use in their own classes, while the pupils enjoy typewriting and look upon the typewriter with marked favor. (184)

Perhaps the most important of these conclusions are Wood and Freeman's last two claims that the typewriter increased the "achievement" of the students, and that the teachers viewed the typewriter as a "valuable" teaching instrument and "approved" of it, while the students "enjoyed" using the typewriter as an educational instrument.

These claims are important because Wood and Freeman's credibility as distinguished professors of education, their systematic, empirical approach to researching the use of the typewriter, and the seemingly exuberant joy with which teachers and students embraced the instrument led to the recommendation that the typewriter should, no, must, be an instrument for promoting the fundamental school subjects. The "Elementary School Typewriter Investigation" cast the typewriter in such a positive and revolutionary light that the typewriter became ingrained in elementary school curricula for the next fifty years. As Ann Cothran and George E. Mason observe forty-five years later, in "The Typewriter: Time-tested Tool for Teaching Reading and Writing" (1978), "Ben D. Wood and Frank N. Freeman in 1932 paved the way for acceptance [of the typewriter] in elementary schools" (171). The legacy of the synthesis of typewriter technology and form-alist pedagogy has shaped the learning patterns, knowledge bases, and identities of millions of students from the 1930s until the present day.

Toulmin Scheme Analysis of
Rhetoric of the Typewriter

It appears that these educators (Mowry, Palmer, Waldo, Rowland, Haefner, Wood and Freeman, and Cothran and Mason) reach the conclusion that the typewriter should be an instrument for promoting the fundamental school subjects based upon the assumptive warrant that writing technology has generally benefited learning and teaching. Mowry, in "The Educational Use of the Typewriter in Schools" (1891), notes that the typewriter has contributed positively to other segments of society, so naturally it should enrich teaching and learning. Mowry writes, "it will readily appear that the typewriter has an important educational mission to fulfill. It is already indispensable to the lawyer, the minister, the literary writer, the editor, the statesman, the merchant, the manufacturer, and now the teacher and the pupil come in for their share, while soon the family will find it a real necessity" (637). For Mowry, capitalism and the trickle-down theory dictate that the typewriter will be invaluable to teachers and students, regardless of the type of pedagogy the typewriter (re)creates or (re)inforces. However, Mowry's reasoning reflects the belief that education is a type of vocational training used to prepare students for contributions to the well-being of society.

Similarly, Ralph Haefner, in *The Typewriter in the Primary and Intermediate Grades: A Basic Educational Instrument for Younger Children* (1932), observes "the place of the typewriter as a basic instrument in the business world is now universally established. Its use in the high school as an important part of the vocational training is also familiar to most people" (3). Haefner concludes that because the typewriter contributed to these segments of society, it should also better elementary school classrooms. Haefner's and Mowry's views of the typewriter as a tool used by many areas of society also hints at the typewriter's shaping of not only students' and teachers' but society's perceptions of the forms and uses of knowledge.

Backing for these generalized warrants can be found in educators' references to historical documentation of technological inventions that have dramatically improved learning, teaching, and society. These technological inventions include the development of written characters, the development of writing materials, the development of mechanical writing instruments, and comparisons to other mechanical inventions. An example of this type of backing can be found in the August 11, 1890 *Chicago Daily Herald*:

> Experiments made with some quite young children show that by use of one of these instruments [the typewriter] they will learn to read, spell and write in less time than they learn to do one of these things under the present methods of instruction. All children delight in using a machine. They are fascinated with an instrument that enables them to print their own names and those of their companions. They do not tire of using it for the reason that it enables them to do a great variety of things. It is possible that the typewriter may accomplish more in increasing intelligence than the printing press has done. It will be a time and labor-saving machine adapted to the acquirement and dissemination of knowledge.

Here, the reference to the printing press helps establish documentation and a tradition of technology influencing learning and teaching practices. Once again, this technology has direct bearing on the types of knowledge society values and uses. The article also suggests students' and society's fascination with the novelty of the typewriter and the power of change it promises.

Palmer, in "Educational Aspects of Typewriting," also draws a connection between the improvements in teaching and technological inventions. Discussing how the typewriter has become a necessity of modern civilization, Palmer comments:

> Quick execution, clear, clean-cut accuracy of expression, these are what the age as a whole, and business men in particular, want and are requiring. The schools must help to secure these results. They *are* helping. The past six months have witnessed a decided advance, both in the actual introduction of machines into the school-room and in the appreciation of their relations to education by leading educators. There are so many advantages that this innovation was from the first as bound to come as was the steam engine after James Watt watched the tea kettle in his mother's kitchen. (624)

Palmer's reference to Scottish inventor James Watt's contribution to the steam engine in the late 1700s establishes another correlation between technology and the bettering of human existence. In addition to this melioristic ideology, Palmer's comparison of the typewriter to the steam engine also reflects industrialism and the expectations of mechanical production.

More backing can be found in Frank Waldo's "The Educational Use of the Typewriter." Waldo makes a comparison between the typewriter and the dictionary and sewing machine. He writes, "without doubt we may look forward to the time when the typewriter will become as much a family necessity as a dictionary or a sewing machine, but it can never fully take the place of the pen on account of its bulkiness and its necessary costliness" (492). By becoming a practical, commonplace object, the typewriter, like the dictionary, would contribute to correct language use and literacy, and, like the sewing machine, enable its users to produce uniform, well-constructed sheets of thought and articles of information.

Like Waldo, Haefner, in *The Typewriter in the Primary and Intermediate Grades: A Basic Educational Instrument for Younger Children*, views the typewriter as a technological invention that will improve learning and teaching. Haefner states, "the development and widespread use of the typewriter during the past sixty years is but a step in the long history of the art of writing. As an instrument for recording thought, the portable machine is a direct descendent of the printing press, the quill pen, the stylus, and the square stick" (3). Haefner's observation that the typewriter's lineage dates back to ancient inventions is an obvious and well-founded one. However, the typewriter is also quite unique. Unlike other personal writing devices, but similar to the printing press, the typewriter provides a means of "standardized" and "form-alized" writing—writing that is easily scanned for surface errors and grammatical and syntactical mistakes. Through these accounts, educators backed their warrant that technology has generally benefited learning and teaching and substantiated their claim that the typewriter should be an instrument for promoting the fundamental, form-alist school subjects.

Form-alist educators' claims were qualified by their beliefs that the typewriter should be used in secondary and college classrooms as a vocational training instrument. This arises from the idea that at the secondary and college level, emphasis should be on correct grammar and language usage, which are skills necessary for careers and adulthood. Two studies at the turn of the century were concerned with vocational uses of the typewriter by adults. Edgar James Swift, in "The Acquisition of Skill in Type-Writing; A Contribution to the Psychology of Learning," reports a study that "was undertaken in the hope of getting further information about some uncertain factors in the learning process" of typing (295). Swift charted his progress, which showed an increase from 350 words typed per hour to 1,100 words typed per hour over a fifty-day period. Four years later, Swift conducted another study, this time collaboratively with William Schuyler. In "The Learning Process," the authors report on the number of errors Schuyler made while learning to type "during each day's practice" for sixty-six consecutive days. Swift and Schuyler marked the mistakes with red ink and found that "the alteration of spotted spaces with those free from marks was striking" (310). This led them to conclude that the "relation of errors to progress in a new line of work calls for further investigation. Such study might show what methods economize time and energy, by disclosing the conditions favorable to errors" (310). Clearly, Swift and Schuyler are concerned with accuracy and efficiency in typewriting—characteristics associated with vocational training and hiring practices.

Through historical research and analysis, educators' promotion and advocacy of the new technology known as the typewriter in elementary school classrooms becomes apparent. However, the deeper, underlying reasons for the advocacy and use of the typewriter still remain unanswered. In the following section, I consider possible reasons why.

Form-al Pedagogy and Rhetoric of the Typewriter

Following the method used in the previous section, I now consider why the typewriter was so readily promoted and advocated as a pedagogical instrument in the elementary school classroom. After analyzing the data, I have come to the conclusion that typewriter use in the classroom reinforced and recreated a form-alist pedagogy. My data for making connections between form-al pedagogy and rhetoric of the typewriter consists of the same material used for the rhetorical analysis of educators' claims about the typewriter. However, I analyze this data from an alternative perspective and with a different purpose. Rather than illustrating the form-alist educators' claim that the typewriter should be an instrument for promoting the fundamental school subjects, I now use this data to consider my conclusion of why the typewriter was used in the elementary school classroom.

One of the earliest examples of educators' reinforcing and recreating form-alist pedagogy through typewriter technology is evident in Mowry's "The Educational Use of the Typewriter in Schools." Mowry asserts:

> [T]hat young persons in school, in learning the art of English composition, should not be troubled with the question *what to say*, but should be required to consider only *how to say it*. This is the true secret of learning how to write. The thought should be given the student, and he should exercise all his powers upon the problem of "how to say it." [. . .] The school boy may acquire the art of accurate and even elegant diction. Primarily, as stated above this comes from familiarity with correctly expressed English. (629)

After establishing a pedagogical agenda, Mowry addresses the most "troublesome part" of teaching, that of overcoming "mechanical obstacles." Elementary school teachers face, Mowry explains, the "great and prolonged trial" of teaching students "what a sentence is: when, where and how to put the period and begin the next sentence with a capital letter; how to spell correctly; how to divide words at the end of a line, and how to use the hyphen; where to place commas and semi-colons; when to use the colon and the dash; and above all, how to divide the matters into paragraphs." Mowry notes that students could "write composition till doomsday, and never learn these things." Mowry then claims this is because students have no guide or template when writing, they are accustomed to reading printed pages, where they see correct spelling, proper punctuation and paragraphs, and correctly constructed sentences. Students take all of these grammatical and syntactical elements for granted when reading—"they see them and pass them by, unconsciously feeling that they are correct, they no not why" (630).

Mowry observes that while facing this dilemma, elementary school teachers were suddenly provided with the possibility of using "the invention of the writing machine, so properly called the Typewriter," in their classrooms. The new technology known as the typewriter:

[M]akes it possible to place in every school room, a little instrument, in compact and convenient form, which can be put upon any ordinary table or desk, where the pupil would lay his paper to write, and, then, sitting erect in a healthful position, and not cramped up, or bending over to get his eyes near to the paper, as in writing, he manipulates the keys, so easily learned, and writes his answer to questions, his written exercises, his composition or whatever he is required to express in good English, in clear, printed type, a language he is accustomed to and understands. (631)

Here is a machine that answers elementary school teachers' woes. Students now have a tool for recreating accurate and legible writing—writing that exhibits well-formed characters, sentences, and paragraphs. In the previous passage, Mowry also anticipates Rowland's third fundamental consideration: "Is it possible that extended practice in typewriting might result in physiological harm to the pupils because of the muscular co-ordinations involved?" (535). Mowry believes the typewriter promotes proper posture and form, liberating students from the backbreaking and tedious monotony of writing by hand. Similarly, Waldo, in "The Educational Use of the Typewriter," predicts "habitual use of the typewriter would increase lung capacity" and improve student posture (486).

Mowry's rhetoric reverberates with industrialist ideology, portraying the writing class as an assembly line of properly formed texts. He writes, "when the first pupil has written his sentences, the next takes the machine, writes his, and then the next, and so on, till the entire class has completed the task. The next day, when the class is called, all have the lesson carefully written, and in type which can be easily corrected, and the errors readily pointed out" (637). Following form-alist pedagogy, the entire class becomes a well-oiled machine, rhythmically reproducing sentence after sentence after sentence.

Palmer, in "Educational Aspects of Typewriting," also reinforces and recreates form-alist pedagogy through typewriter technology. Palmer interviewed several leading educators who had experience using the typewriter in the classroom, analyzed their testimony, and summarized the benefits the typewriter held for education. He concludes, "with remarkable unanimity [the interviewed educators] bear witness to the advantages growing out of [the typewriter's] use in connection with education, especially as a purely educational instrument, apart from its industrial value" (625). Palmer summarizes these advantages as follows:

1. Rapidity of thought, composition and execution.
2. Accuracy, including careful attention to spelling, punctuation, capitalization, paragraphing, and all rhetorical principles.
3. Neatness.
4. Clearness of thought.
5. Mastery of language, the acquirement of a clear, vigorous English style, including knowledge of the real meaning of words and skill in using them.
6. A great saving of time and strength to the teacher resulting from the superior legibility of examination papers, etc. This means more and better teaching in schools where typewriters are introduced. (625)

Palmer emphasizes practical and stylistic aspects of the typewriter—efficiency, accuracy, and neatness, and also lists two seemingly epistemological categories—"clearness of thought" and "knowledge of the real meaning of words." Disappointingly, Palmer does not elaborate further on these advantages.

Perhaps the most powerful examples of educators' reinforcing and recreating form-alist pedagogy through typewriter technology are evident in the conclusions of the "Elementary School Typewriter Investigation." Haefner, in *The Typewriter in the Primary and Intermediate Grades: A Basic Educational Instrument for Younger Children*, summarizes these in four broad categories: the language activities and the typewriter; an early means of writing; a rapid means of writing; and a means of producing orderly papers (18). Addressing "the language activities and the typewriter," Haefner notes that "even a very superficial consideration" of the typewriter reveals that it uses the same sort of printed characters a student encounters in books created with movable type printing presses. Similarly, the typewriter "calls for the same attention to the selection and arrangement of letters as is basic to correct spelling [. . .] [i]t is constructed in such a way as to facilitate many of the important mechanical requirements of written composition [. . .] [and] [i]t enables the child to prepare written compositions which can be read orally with ease and expression" (18). In "an early means of writing," Haefner notes "the machine provides the child with a means of doing clear writing, long before he has achieved a practical mastery of the more difficult handwriting." Haefner believes students' abilities to produce "clear-cut" words and numerals has obvious advantages in connection with "reading, spelling, and composition, as well as arithmetic" (18). In "a rapid means of writing," Haefner notes that "The effect of greater speed will tend to provide the pupil with more composition practice. It may further be supposed that it would give the writing itself a flexibility and spontaneity which a slower means of execution might not provide" (18). In this seemingly contradictory statement, Haefner recounts the standard form-alist praise of the typewriter's speed and efficiency, while also hypothetically praising its contribution to "flexibility and spontaneity." Lastly, in "a means of producing orderly papers," Haefner writes that:

> Difficulties in handwriting, in composition mechanics, and in spelling often combine to make attractively prepared papers almost impossible. It may be expected that the typewriter will render easier a number of mechanical features of composition, such as indentation, capitalization, punctuation, and spelling. It lends itself particularly well to careful placing of titles, to combinations of text and pictures, and to systematic outlining. (18)

Haefner, ingrained in form-alist ideology and pedagogy, capitalizes upon and stresses the typewriter's ability to create visually appealing, stylistically proper writing. By providing students with a means of producing mechanically correct writing, educators strengthen not only their methods of teaching, but also their beliefs in the concerns of teaching.

In his description and recommendations for classroom applications of the typewriter, Haefner repeatedly uses metaphors that illustrate form-alist educators' pedagogy and the expected role of the typewriter. For example, Haefner writes:

> The complete grasp of the function of an instrument is an important phase of learning to control it. The novice in car driving has to learn, not only how to operate the various levers and brakes, but also which to operate under varying conditions. It helps him very little to know that he moves his foot, if he does not remember what will happen when he moves it in

a certain way. The function of the typewriter can be grasped by the young child, not only in its totality but in its details. He finds that a certain part of the machine holds the paper, another moves it, another makes the mark, another spaces between words, and that a combination of these devices makes writing possible. (48)

For Haefner, and other form-alist educators, the act of writing becomes embodied in the mechanisms of the typewriter. The paper, the keyboard, the type bars, the ink ribbon, the carriage, the shift key, the margin release, the clatter are all now part of the creative and critical thinking process of writing. Even if in his metaphors Haefner implies and hopes students will become one with the machine and achieve freedom; however, the cold, mechanical exercises Haefner recommends for students negates this. Typical exercises include, "Copying printed material for which they have use," "Writing lists of various kinds, such as spelling words," and "Planning and typing a table of contents, a book cover, or a heading for a magazine page" (90).

Toulmin Scheme Analysis of Form-al Pedagogy and Rhetoric of the Typewriter

My claim that typewriter use in the classroom reinforced and recreated form-al ideology and pedagogy is warranted by the general statement that advocacy of technology often reflects current ideologies and pedagogies. This is backed by similarities between the introduction of the typewriter to classrooms and Walter J. Ong's inquiry into the relationship between the movable type printing press and Ramistic pedagogy, and Gail Hawisher, et al.'s examination of the interactions between the computer, the current-traditionalist paradigm, and the writing process movement.

Backing for my claim about typewriter technology follows a continuing pattern in the inextricable and historical melding of ideology, technology, and pedagogy. One of the most powerful examples of this dynamic interplay is the invention and improvement of the movable type printing press, beginning in the fourteenth century, and the "place-logic" version of humanism promoted by Rudolph Agricola and Peter Ramus, beginning in the 1480s. As Ong notes in *Ramus, Method, and the Decay of Dialogue* the printing press was "an advance of the same importance as that of the invention of the alphabet itself" (308). Ramus's method of learning, teaching, and representing logic through a dichotomized arrangement of material telescoping from locus to loci to further loci and so on was relatively easy to print and distribute. Ong writes, "The diagrammatic tidiness which printing was imparting to the realm of ideas was part of a large-scale operation freeing the book from the world of discourse and making it over into an object, a box with surface and 'content' like an Agricolan locus or a Ramist argument or a Cartesian or Lockean idea" (311).

Ramus's method of organizing knowledge according to spatial models was closely associated with the use of letterpress printing in educational circles. Once printed textbooks became available for classroom use, the teacher was able to focus lessons on the spatial arrangement of material before the students. Ong describes the teaching environment such technology cultivated: "'Look at page seven, line three, the fourth word'—this kind of directive became a matter of daily routine in a typographical culture. Millions of schoolboys were inducted into an understanding of language and of the world around them by making their way conjointly through individual texts arranged in identical spatial patterns" (313).

Before the invention of the movable type printing press, when each book was unique and characterized by individuality, such directives were unrealistic. Ramistic ideology and pedagogy, when combined with the new technology of the printing press, focused writing instruction on correct grammar and language usage.

Another ideological, technological, and pedagogical matrix is apparent in the computer revolution of the 1970s and the tension between the current-traditionalist paradigm and the writing process movement beginning in the 1970s. Hawisher, et al., in *Computers and the Teaching of Writing in American Higher Education, 1979–1994: A History*, observe that, "[c]omputers entered the writing scene at a moment when there was a loud and public call for the improvement of writing instruction, and at the beginning of what was to be a long and difficult period of reentrenchment in American public education" (23). Richard Young and Maxine Hairston characterize the ideological movement from a focus on the written product to a concern with the writing process as a paradigm shift. However, this paradigm shift is by no means complete. "The paradigm shift may have occurred in the pages of our journals, but it had not occurred in many, and perhaps in most, American writing classrooms" (Hawisher, et al. 31). Writing process advocates, such as Donald Murray and Peter Elbow, spoke of three stages or activities—prewriting, writing, and revising *or* rehearsing, drafting, and revising. A fourth stage, proofreading or copyediting, was rarely mentioned. Proponents of the writing process praised the recursiveness of the computer but were wary of the current-traditionalists' emphasis on the computer as style checker. Hawisher, et al. write that the "continuing interest in the computer as style checker suggests that the current-traditional paradigm, and its interest in 'product,' is far from dead. It also suggests that the Writing Process paradigm shaped the ways in which style checkers would be viewed and used in the field" (31). The present use and understanding of the new computer technology in writing pedagogy is a synthesis of ideologies from the current-traditionalist paradigm and the writing process movement. This has resulted not only in the dilemma surrounding the role of the computer in writing pedagogy but also the purpose of composition in education—the dichotomized question of whether writing instruction should focus on correct grammar and language usage or heuristic activities.

Ong's research into the connections between the movable type printing press and Ramistic pedagogy and Hawisher, et al.'s inquiry into the interactions between the computer, the current-traditionalist paradigm, and the writing process movement clearly establish the necessity for seeking understanding of the synthesis of technology, ideology, and pedagogy. The advocacy of the typewriter by form-alist educators at the turn of the century represents another crucial component in the history and future of education.

Obviously, numerous qualifiers and rebuttals exist to the claim that typewriter use in the classroom reinforced and recreated form-al ideology and pedagogy. Waldo, in "The Educational Use of the Typewriter," alludes to the possibility that the typewriter, through its standardized production of letters, might free teachers and students from the arduous task of concentrating on handwriting, and instead focus on ideas. Waldo writes:

> The widespread use of the typewriter has introduced a new standard, or at least very much modified the old standard of judgment of individuality based upon written productions. Editors have heretofore divided their attention between the chirography and the substance of the written page, but the

typewritten copy allows all the power judgment to be directed towards the substance itself. (489)

This notion that the typewriter will allow students and teachers to take for granted the formation of legible and well-written words, and subsequently allow them to focus on "the substance itself," the ideas, thoughts, or concepts, is a noble one. However, under form-alist pedagogy, this was not the purpose of the typewriter.

Another possible qualifier is apparent in Rowland's "An Experiment in Teaching Touch Typewriting to Pupils in the Fifth and Sixth Grades." Rowland suggests the typewriter "creates a love of order, neatness, and symmetry; that it aids in teaching the great essentials of English composition; that it improves ability in spelling and reading; that it furnishes an opportunity of the imagination to express itself and develops the creative instinct; that it develops habits of accuracy and concentration; etc." (533). Yet another qualifier is evident in the student examples from Haefner's *The Typewriter in the Primary and Intermediate Grades: A Basic Educational Instrument for Younger Children*. These examples show that creative and even heuristic use of the typewriter by the students was evident, but seemed suppressed by the mechanical constraints of the typewriter and the form-alist pedagogy. Nevertheless, many of the "pictures" typed by students are striking, innovative, and highly complex.

THE NEXT MACHINE

My inquiry and analysis into rhetoric of the typewriter thus far represents a preliminary step. Future exploration of the topic might include analyzing form-alist educators' warrants. Andrew Feenberg, in *Critical Theory of Technology*, contends that "technology is subservient to values established in other social spheres" (5), that technology is a tool society uses in various ways to support existing cultural practices, and that technology influences and creates epistemological and ontological aspects of society. By analyzing rhetoric of the typewriter using Feenberg's perspectives, technology becomes an effective vehicle for pedagogy, a vital part of a larger social mechanism for reproducing certain pedagogies, and even a method for understanding ways of seeing blind teachers, educators, and students to other ways of knowing.

Additionally, a large scale comparison of the influences of key technological writing inventions throughout history seems extremely valuable for understanding the continuing relationships between technology, pedagogy, and ideology. A meta-analysis of the connections between Ong's work with the movable type printing press and Ramistic pedagogy, the interactions between the typewriter and form-alist pedagogy, and the relations between computer technology and current writing pedagogy would contribute to a better understanding of our students, ourselves, and our next machine.

WORKS CITED

Bizzell, Patricia, and Bruce Herzberg, eds. *The Rhetorical Tradition*. Boston, MA: Bedford, 1990. Print.

Cothran, Ann, and George E. Mason. "The Typewriter: Time-tested Tool for Teaching Reading and Writing." *Elementary School Journal* 78 (1978): 171–173. Print.

Feenberg, Andrew. *Critical Theory of Technology*. New York: Oxford UP, 1991. Print.

—. *Questioning Technology*. New York: Routledge, 1999. Print.

Haefner, Ralph. *The Typewriter in the Primary and Intermediate Grades: A Basic Instrument for Younger Children*. New York: Macmillan, 1932. Print.

Hawisher, Gail, Paul LeBlanc, Charles Moran, and Cynthia L. Selfe. *Computers and the Teaching of Writing in American Higher Education, 1979–1994: A History*. New Jersey: Ablex, 1996. Print.

Mowry, William A. "The Educational Use of the Typewriter in Schools." *Education* XI (1891): 625–637. Print.

Ong, Walter J. *Ramus, Method, and the Decay of Dialogue*. Cambridge, MA: Harvard UP, 1958. Print.

Palmer, Frank H. "Educational Aspects of Typewriting." *Education* XII (1892): 622–629. Print.

Rowland, Ralph S. "An Experiment in Teaching Touch Typewriting to Pupils in the Fifth and Sixth Grades." *Elementary School Journal* XXX (1930): 533–538. Print.

Swift, Edgar James. "The Acquisition of Skill in Type-Writing; A Contribution to the Psychology of Learning." *The Psychological Bulletin* I (1904): 295–305. Print.

Swift, Edgar James, and William Schuyler. "The Learning Process." *The Psychological Bulletin* IV (1907): 307–310. Print.

Toulmin, Stephen. *The Uses of Argument*. London: Cambridge UP, 1958. Print.

Waldo, Frank. "The Educational Use of the Typewriter." *Education* XXII (1902): 484–492. Print.

Wood, Ben D., and Frank N. Freeman. *An Experimental Study of the Educational Influences of the Typewriter in the Elementary School Classroom.* New York: Macmillan, 1932. Print.

5 Handwriting, Literacy, and Technology

Kathleen Blake Yancey

ACT ONE: THE INHERITANCE OF HANDWRITING

The thing you'd notice about my mother was her beautiful handwriting, the kind of handwriting suggesting a beauty born of order and symmetry, a penmanship whose regular features spoke to a good earth, a world at peace, a universe where everyone's home was a clean, well-lit place. Born in 1924 in San Mateo, California, she was the elder daughter of two. Her mother had grown up on a Montana ranch, the only girl in a family of cowboys whose first move as an adult was to join the Red Cross and sail with the USO to help soldiers in Europe during World War I, war or no war, ladylike or not. To Montana, she never returned. She met my grandfather, one of some eight siblings (or was it eleven? They were never very good at keeping count) raised on an Illlinois farm, a lawyer who didn't finish law school, preferring simply to pass the bar exam. He didn't seem to like country life much either, making his way west to San Francisco, which in those days was still recovering from the 1906 earthquake. Their handwriting was of their time, my grandmother's not much prettier than her name, Olive, though certainly serviceable enough, and as a child I loved it as a sign of who she was—my grandma, she of the short stature, baker of the sweetest cookies, fashion designer and seamstress of the most elegant doll clothes. In that handwriting, I heard

> We should not study handwriting as a phenomenon that reflects changing conceptions of the self but as one of the places where the self happened.
>
> —*Handwriting in America*

her raspy voice, a sandpaper sound I identify as hers even today. The thing you'd say about my father's handwriting is that it was terrible, not in the merely ugly sense of the word terrible, although it was that, just ugly, but terrible in the sense that it was uncontrolled, disjointed, laborious, from letter to letter incoherent. Through that handwriting, *he* looked illiterate. Born in 1922 (which every year seems closer

> Since the 18th century [. . .] handwriting has functioned as a way to define and reveal the self. In the ways that we have taught handwriting, practiced it, and perceived it, we have tried both to shape what we ought to be and to express what we hope to be.
>
> —*The History of Handwriting*

to a century ago), the younger of two brothers, raised in the city of San Francisco, he was assigned the daily task of sweeping forty-nine stairs on the back of the house. Detail was his middle name. His mother had grown up in San Jose, where the San Francisco earthquake had spread, and his father had seen the city firsthand from the time he was a boy. These grandparents were the elegant ones, with an apartment by the Bay, silver and linens at every meal, a doorman to let us in. My grandmother's hand was like her, elegant, with strokes that were narrow, curls dipping teasingly below the line, oversized capitals authoritatively announcing the commencement of paragraphs. Nana's letters to me lent me her class.

The thing about all this handwriting is that it both made sense and didn't, even to me as a child. At the risk of sounding like a graphologist, my one grandmother's handwriting was work(wo)manlike, as was she; the other's almost calligraphy-like in ways that, to my mind, expressed her—well, essence. On the other hand my parents' handwriting seemed a reverse image of their behavior. My mother, a Democrat, a full-time homemaker, a person who not only tolerated chaos but also often created it, expressed herself in a handwriting organized and serene. My father, a Republican, an administrator for the government, an organized, neat person, at the end of the day a practicing agnostic about nearly everything but discipline, expressed himself through a handwriting incoherent in its illegible scribble. How could their handwriting so mislead us about who they were? Alternatively, what do we make of my question: is it reasonable—or merely naïve—to expect one's handwriting to provide a clue as to someone's personality?[1]

Even as a child, I had asked my mother about her handwriting, hoping mine could magically become like hers, and she'd replied,

"Palmer method." Somehow I thought this method was technology-light, a handwritten script one repeated until it took hold; so with enough practice, I thought, the Palmer method could transform my handwriting into something like my mother's, and had I begun early enough, it might have. That was precisely its promise. What I didn't understand was twofold. One: when my mother and her peers learned to write, it was cursive first and always. Unlike the practice today wherein children first learn print and then cursive, my mother and her peers learned cursive first and only. I never saw my mother print— this observation is itself an interesting comment on literacy and how we conceive of it. Two: the Palmer method was a serious technology imposing a serious discipline, forming exactly in the way I (first) admired, but achieving its effects through a uniformity of behavior that was literally mindless, at the time called "automatic." Acquiring a Palmer "hand" required a specific, repetitive labor intended to produce a consistent result of special value to the business community as well as to pedagogues:

> Mr. Palmer promised to deliver a tireless arm that could compete with the typewriter, but what really attracted educators were his handwriting drills. Any survivor of these drills will be happy to describe them to you. Sometimes they began with "preparatory calisthenics." Then, at the teacher's command (educators recommended using phrases such as "At Attention!" and "Present Arms!"), students executed row after row of ovals and "push-pulls." School officials were blunt about the value of these drills. The lessons they conveyed—conformity to standard models, obedience to authority—would reform juvenile delinquents, assimilate foreigners, and acclimate working-class children to their futures in the typing pool or on the factory line. (Thornton "History")

This handwriting, in other words, which enabled one to compete with the typewriter, did so by instilling a discipline compatible with a process of socialization that, ironically, would assimilate at the same time it maintained class segregation.

So why, I might ask, was my father's handwriting so unruly? He was educated at the same time and in the same variety of Catholic schools as my mother, but he had one distinct disadvantage: he was left-handed. Historically, left-handers have been stigmatized and shunned:

A left-hander was supposed to be not only unlucky, but also awkward and clumsy, as shown in the French *gauche*, and adroit, droit meaning right, and adroit meaning skilled. German *links* and *linkisch* and the Dutch expression "twee linkerhanden hebben" ("to have two left hands," which means being clumsy). As these are all very old words, they support theories indicating that the predominance of right-handedness is an extremely old phenomenon.

One might say that since my father was able to access school, conditions for lefties had improved. One might also observe, however, that the perceptions about lefties were made true by enforcing a right-handedness that never became natural or subject to control, and as the handwriting went, so too life.[2]

ACT TWO: ECHOES OF THE PRESENT TENSE

In *Handwriting in America*, a cultural study of the role handwriting has played in the US, Tamara Thornton observes that handwriting "inscribes" the self. Handwriting, put differently, is itself a technology that takes a diversity of forms, but always with a specific, defining effect, whether for expressing the self or for corralling the masses. Interestingly, the story of my grandparents' and parents' handwriting is the story of these two ways of understanding handwriting. Collectively, my parents and theirs lived at the nexus of a major shift in conceptualizing handwriting, with profound implications for generations of writers in the twentieth century as the pendulum shifted from handwriting-qua-self to handwriting-qua-labor. In terms of my own family, my grandparents were the product of Victorian notions of handwriting whereas my parents were the products of a more "progressive" time:

> Victorians had placed their hopes in the will as the ultimate source of social order, but consciousness of any sort had a way of getting out of hand, of working toward ends other than those envisioned by educators. The new conception of the learning process, steeped in the new psychology of the early twentieth century, either ignored consciousness or denied its existence. Educators now called for bodies to be disciplined, nowhere more so than in handwriting instruction. Thus ed-

ucators claimed that the penmanship regimen, in asserting control of the 'student body,' would yield important social benefits. It would reform delinquents, assimilate foreigners, and shape a workforce. (Thornton 144)

This shift in both understandings of and instruction in handwriting was also, in part, a function of a new sense of education-qua-science that, ironically, forecasts the current educational climate—with its emphasis on sorting students by testing them and by developing new testing technologies that would make possible and efficient large-scale efforts to do so.[3] Moreover, this shift, previously neglected in composition studies' histories of writing assessment, accounts for the first such large-scale effort in schools, one where academics specializing in education could hone their new "scientific" research skills.

> In the first quarter of the twentieth century, academics offered their help. Their efforts led them into three related areas of inquiry: how best to write, how best to teach writing, and how to measure the results of that instruction. Should all students use Palmer's 'whole- arm movement,' or were there more efficient ways of writing? Might these methods vary from individual to individual? What about left-handedness? Did Palmer's ovals and push-pulls (arm-movement drills), or any kind of drill, make pedagogical sense? And finally, how could educators test pupils to evaluate their levels of handwriting achievement? (Thornton 145)

Here, the question of how to test is directly related to how to teach, all located in the context of "pedagogical sense."

George Hillocks has commented on the relation of form to content in the teaching of writing—arguing that to the detriment of student learning, we teach form rather than content—but the early twentieth-century version of handwriting instruction predates and anticipates an analogous conflation. As the twentieth century opened, handwriting *was* writing, an equation whose implementation yoked one's ability to form correct letters to one's ability to compose. Much as in the case of grammar today—when grammar is identified *as* writing—writing itself had no status or conception apart from handwriting, as noted writing scholar Donald Graves explains based on his own experience: "Handwriting was one of those early school experiences I have tried to repress. . . . Recollections of endless circles, precise spacing, and comments about my untidiness take away my energy. *I had no idea that handwriting was for writing. . . .*" (emphasis added, Thornton 188). Instruction in handwriting was also, as instruction in reading and writing are today, accompanied by remedial instruction for those who failed. As remembered by Jack McGarvey, remedial education then was not much different than today:

> My papers were always returned covered with directions for more cursive practice. . . . So while most of the other kids got to play with white paste, I spent my time with eyes turned upward, meditating upon the charts of perfect cursive above the chalkboards. I tried hard to copy what I saw, but no amount of practice helped. And because my cursive was unattractive, I thought I had nothing to say. My teacher agreed. (Thornton 189)

Inscribing the self here equates beauty, always a cultural construct, with the intelligence of a particular person. Moreover, much like students today who are denied education in the arts so that they can practice for retests in so-called basic skills, McGarvey's curriculum is circumscribed by his "failure" at handwriting. Perhaps most important, it's not only that the teacher literally sees McGarvey through his handwriting but also that McGarvey sees himself through the same lens.

Defining failure by psychometric methods was, of course, another addition to the new education of the early twentieth century. Edward Thorndike, who is credited with making intelligence testing a mainstay of many institutions (including the Army), created a scale for handwriting in 1909; its values were "beauty and character as well as legibility" (Freeman 218). Although this handwriting scale wasn't the only one available, the Thorndike Writing Scale became "the first popular standardized achievement test used in the public schools. A wide variety of achievement and aptitude tests quickly followed" (Perrone). The "academic experts" were not displeased to have this help. They

> saw many uses for handwriting scales. They argued that standardized tests would motivate students to improve their penmanship. If a competitive spirit took over, so much the better. The writing scale would also be used to establish quantitative standards of achievement. Pupils would have to take note of minimum standards for satisfactory completion of a grade

> level, while teachers would need to ensure that their students
> as a whole met standards for classroom-wide averages. Mean-
> while, quantitative comparisons of one class with another
> could be used to figure out what methods were most effec-
> tive or, by the same token, which individual instructors and
> schools were substandard. Tests tested pupils, but they also
> tested teachers. (Thornton 149)

With handwriting came testing, and once testing of one skill became
a way to motivate students and monitor teachers, testing became not
an adjunct to education, but a central practice whose influence accelerated with alarming alacrity.

> By the 1930s, a majority of schools in the United States and
> Canada engaged in some form of standardized testing, but
> the scope was exceedingly small by today's standards. Few
> people who completed high school before 1950, for example,
> took more than three standardized tests in their entire school
> careers. The results were hardly ever discussed, parents didn't
> receive the scores and school-wide results were not grist for
> local newspapers. By contrast to this earlier period, those who
> complete[d] high school in 1991 will have taken, on average,
> from 18 to 21 standardized tests; many will have taken more,
> the majority of them in the K-5 years. And test scores will not
> only fill newspapers, but also become part of the sales-pitch
> of real estate brokers, especially if test scores are high in a par-
> ticular district. To understand the overall magnitude of the
> shift, it should be noted that since 1950 the volume of test-
> ing has grown at the annual rate of 10–20 percent (Haney &
> Madaus, 1989). (Perrone)

The introduction of a new labor-based handwriting in schools is
linked to a new practice, testing, which during the course of less than
a century would come to dominate schools. With help from scholars like Thorndike and enthusiasm for a more regular and regulated
education, testing was seen as both possible and desirable. Ironically,
although handwriting was understood as writing, and although scales
and human judgment provided the foundation for the testing of handwriting, this testing technology would not be used in the testing of
composing for decades, and only then reluctantly.

ACT THREE: BACK TO THE FUTURE

As James Porter has noted, technology matters to writing, an observation evidenced daily if not hourly in the digital age. What's less obvious—and in fact is difficult to see because it's ubiquitous and thus invisible—is that technology matters to handwriting at least as much. In 2005, Doug Hesse raised a related question, "Who Owns Writing?" and we might well append that question to ask, who owns handwriting? Putting these questions and observations together, we might anticipate handwriting's quiet exit from the educational stage, especially in light of the fact that testing is now beginning to replace the hand with the keyboard. In the 2011 National Assessment of Educational Progress (NAEP), eighth and twelfth graders will compose at the screen, using handwriting—if at all—for notes and quick drafts. A growing body of personal and public evidence, however, suggests that handwriting is likely not to disappear, but to maintain and perhaps increase its status, in part as a consequence of digital technologies that merely remediate the old, and perhaps not surprisingly, in part because of testing.

My son is a graduate student in math, having earned a BS in computer engineering and a BS in math, having won the Layman prize for best math essay in his graduating year, having published not one but two articles as an undergraduate. Apparently, he can write; but he does not write cursive except for his signature—he prints. His history explains why, I think. In Montessori kindergarten, he learned to read, but didn't pursue handwriting other than in letters of sand. In first grade, he wrote with invented spelling—and he was sufficiently inventive that he was the only person who could translate it. His words were often incorrectly spelled, and he didn't use spaces to separate words. In second grade, he met the late twentieth century version of McGarvey's teacher, who was most seriously displeased with Matt and with his handwriting. She saw them as the same. First, she attempted to demonstrate that he was learning disabled, and when no evidence of that could be discovered, she sent him to an occupational therapist, which given that Matt was seven, seemed a little extreme. His occupation, after all, was learning. Yet since he got out of class, Matt thought the visit with the therapist a treat, especially since the therapist was young and interested in him. They visited three times before inviting me to join them. Worried, I asked her diagnosis. Her reply: "Let's get the teacher off his back." Although Matt was luckier than McGarvey in that no other teacher mistook his handwriting for his self, the point remains. He prints.

Oddly, recent and forthcoming tests continue an emphasis on technology, and currently, on at least some tests, the technology of choice is handwriting. Tests today are not often used to enforce handwriting as in the early twentieth century, but handwriting-as-medium-for-writing progressively links if not conflates the two. It's almost a return to 1909 when the two were co-identified. The most recent example of a test moving to include writing is the SAT, whose writing test is one-third "direct measure" writing and two-thirds multiple choice. The student's handwritten text is scanned so that it can be distributed electronically (to raters, to college admissions offices, etc.). While other tests of writing such as that included in the Advanced Placement haven't highlighted the medium, the "new" SAT one has, in part because it is using digital technology in its scanning, thus inherently raising the issue of technology, and in equal part because of its perceived impact on college admissions. Such impact raises the anxiety level for students and parents already worried, nowhere more so than for students intending to become doctors, who themselves are notorious for their illegible hand. In other words, in the instance of the new SAT, we see a perfect storm of anxiety in which the bar to medical practice, and by extension to other professions, seems to have been raised—because of handwriting. Put another way, as the College Board explains, *how* a student (hand) writes is every bit as important as what she or he writes:

> Written production is a huge part of our children's classroom experience. They are expected to write from kindergarten on to demonstrate their understanding of concepts and text in all subject areas. Standardized testing including the MSA and SAT now include written responses. To ensure academic success, it is important that young children develop solid foundational skills. (np, *My Handwriting Helper*)

> Your essay must be written on the lines provided on your answer sheet — you will receive no other paper on which to write. You will have enough space if you write on every line, avoid wide margins, and keep your handwriting to a reasonable size. Remember that people who are not familiar with your handwriting will read what you write. Try to write or print so that what you are writing is legible to those readers. (np)

Anxiety, of course, was at the root of the Palmer method and scientific education, which provided a means of disciplining those who otherwise would be out of control.

The case of medical practice, however, provides a lens through which we can see a continuing source of anxiety related to handwriting. While a doctor's hand may serve as the butt of jokes, medical illegibility is no laughing matter. As *TIME Magazine* reports,

> Doctors' sloppy handwriting kills more than 7,000 people annually. It's a shocking statistic, and, according to a July 2006 report from the National Academies of Science's Institute of Medicine (IOM), preventable medication mistakes also injure more than 1.5 million Americans annually. Many such errors result from unclear abbreviations and dosage indications and illegible writing on some of the 3.2 billion prescriptions written in the U.S. every year. (Caplan)

The anxiety here seems well-placed, and ironically, even for professional practice and in the age of digital technologies, handwriting is still a technology of choice. For one thing, doctors—like other information workers who need to communicate with others—rely on a variegated set of literacy materials, from notes to Post-its, and there is a school of thought among some doctors suggesting that two factors- -the writing by hand about the interaction with patients and the *avoidance* of digital technologies--are critical for quality care:

> Writing in a personal and independent way forces us [doctors] to think and formulate our ideas. Notes that are meant to be focused have become voluminous and template, distracting from the key cognitive work of providing care. Such charts may satisfy the demands of third-party payors, but they are the product of a word-processor, not of physicians' thoughtful review and analysis. They may be "efficient" for the purpose of documentation but not creative thinking." These authors . . . described doctors who used scarce time with patients fixed on their computer screen. . . . (Reiser 99)

The practices recommended by these physician-researchers all rely on an untemplated surface materialand the handwritten form. And at some level, the reaction of these doctors speaks to the power of any technology: "Such problems [as how and in what form to compose notes] reflect the ablity of a powerful technology to channel users along particular paths of inquiry and action, which may not always achive clinical outcomes that best serve patients' interests." (Reiwer 100).

Interestingly, a source of the researcher-doctors' resistance is the *computer screen* itself, which is increasingly taking the form of the tablet or IPAD, and whose purposeis to replicate the technology of handwriting with an eye toward making it more efficient. As the website MedicalTablet optimistically promises, handwritten notes composed with *the digital pen* are the notes that can best serve patients:

> A picture or sketch is worth a thousand words when communicating treatment plans or injury descriptions with your patient. Patients internalize and retain information better through interactive tools. Adding handwritten notes, sketches, and images is easy with the digital pen and handwriting capability. (np)

And medical doctors aren't alone: a chemist I worked with at Clemson loved his tablet because it allowed *even more* handwriting, such as on his student's PowerPoint slides, which, ironically, sometimes prompts the same complaint from students that we hear with paper. I can't read your writing.

Digital technologies, in these scenes, aren't replacing handwriting; they are authorizing it anew.

Epilogue

I began this meditation by reflecting on my parents and grandparents and their writing, at once predictable and surprising. Upon closer glance, though, even the surprises weren't. Like other artifacts and behaviors, handwriting is shaped by culture. However, what's as important, for them as for us, is the reverse: the force of handwriting, its power as a technology to shape us, typically invisibly, often distorting what is, leaves in its wake much more and often worse than a poor hand. Evidence of this resides in the lives of millions of twentieth century Americans; evidence of this is in the educational testing industry beginning with a set of "scientific" scales for a handwriting they confused with writing; evidence of handwriting affecting life through tests every time a student writes the SAT writing test; evidence of this takes new form in the computerized handwritten notes recording our medical histories.

I like handwriting. I like being able to meditate on and reflect on the handwriting of my grandmothers. I like the textured literacy (and its practices) to which handwriting contributes. I don't think I'd want to lose that.

But.

My father, like others before him, was forced to write in a method that cripples.

My son prints.

And this is all evidence—and a technology—to which we should attend.

NOTES

1. This question, of course, is at the heart of forensic handwriting analysis.

2. Lefties are under less duress today, but prejudice and technology still seem leveraged against them. There are exceptions, however. A common technological implementation favoring left-handers is the English-language QWERTY keyboard layout. Since this layout contains far more of the common English letters on the left side of the keyboard, the left hand does a majority of the typing, giving left-handed typists an advantage. This was done because mechanical typewriters would jam if the typer hit too many keys too quickly.The Birth, Death, and Life of Typewriters, np)

3. Williamson's fine article on the workshop of efficiency in writing assessment fails to address the role of handwriting in contributing to such aspirations for efficiency; such efficiency, as the discussion regarding efficiency in the practice of medicine indicates, continues to drive technologies, often at the expense of social relations and of our humanity.

WORKS CITED

Birth, Death, and Life of Typewriters. May 23, 2011. Web.

Caplan, Jeremy. "Cause of Death: Sloppy Doctors." *Time.com.* 15 January 2007. Web. 28 July 2011.

College Board. "The Essay." The SAT. 2011. Web. 13 September 2011.

Freeman, Frank N. "New Handwriting Scale." *The Elementary School Journal* 59.4 (1959): 218–21. Print.

Hesse, Douglas D. "Who Owns Writing?" *College Composition and Communciation* 57.2 (2005): 335–357. Print.

Medical Tablet PC. "Five Medical Practice Tasks Simplified—from Desk to Diagnosis—Using the Tablet PC." 2011. Web. 13 September 2011.

My Handwriting Helper: Pediatric Occupational Therapy Handwriting Coaching Services. 2011. Web. 13 September 2011.

Perrone, Vito. ACEI Position Paper on Standardized Testing. 1991. Web. 7 March 2011.

Reiser, Stanley Joel. *Technological Medicine: The Changing World of Doctors and Patients.* Cambridge: Cambridge UP, 2009.

Thornton, Tamara. *Handwriting in America: A Cultural History.* New Haven: Yale UP, 1998.New Haven, CT: Yale UP, 1998.

Thornton, Tamara. "The History of Handwriting: Handwriting in America." *UB Today.* 1998. Web. 28 July 2011.

Williamson, Michael. The Worship of Efficiency: Untangling Theoretical and Practical Considerations in Writing Assessment. *Assessing Writing* 1 (1994); 147-73.

6 "Making the Devil Useful": Audio-Visual Aids and the Teaching of Writing

Joseph Jones

The comprehensive public high school developed during the first few decades of the twentieth century and became the primary site of writing instruction for American adolescents. English was instituted as a school subject in large measure to develop in students the sort of writing skills colleges deemed necessary. The Committee of Ten, headed by Harvard President Charles Eliot, convened in 1892 to delineate the subject matters for secondary schools. Within a few years, however, many in the schools challenged the Committee's curricular recommendations on the grounds that they were rooted in a decidedly collegiate perspective of the subject of English. Some of those working in high school English studies began viewing their educational mission as broader and more inclusive than only preparing students for college.

Teachers in the emergent high school sought to answer a most basic curricular question: What is English? They sought a definition by identifying purposes apart from, but also including, college preparation. Secondary school teachers may have been the de facto inheritors of a rhetorical tradition, though that term never appears in their professional literature, but they did not inherit a univocal description of why or how writing should be taught. An article in the inaugural issue of *The English Journal* in 1912 captures some of their sense of confusion: "There seems to be a general feeling that the English course is in a chaotic condition, and that something needs to be done about it. [. . .] What is traditional in the present course belongs to a time when the aim of the schools was to prepare the pupils for college. What is new is frequently but a blind attempt to meet the demands of changed conditions not thoroughly understood" (Coulter 24).

Historical records indicate a struggle among those who sought to shape the subject of high school English. There were indeed adherents of the recommendations of the Committee of Ten who conceived high school English primarily in its relation to college English studies. They considered the central goal of secondary school writing instruction to be the production of error-free prose and endorsed a pedagogy founded on drill and exercise. There were other voices in curriculum development, however, that talked of secondary school English as an enterprise distinct from college preparation. For some, that meant emphasizing vocational skills and job preparation, and they designed writing instruction for practical courses such as "Business English." Others argued for a curriculum informed by child development that structured experiences to develop the potential of each student according to his or her particular talents and abilities. Nevertheless, for most high school English teachers, writing instruction was taught in the context of literature, though the emphases in literature shifted from analysis and history toward literary appreciation and meaningful personal responses to literary texts.

It was during this rich period of development and contention that "educational technology" emerged, and it emerged in ways in secondary schools that outpaced its emergence in American colleges. Many in secondary schools were eager to experiment with technology, and their efforts instantiate their concerns, aspirations, struggles, and missteps at creating the subject of English. Reviewing the writings of teachers from the first few decades of the twentieth century reveal that high school English teachers then––and now, for that matter––are tasked with an educational mission in flux, under constant scrutiny, and subject always to revision and expansion. Furthermore, as high school English teachers in the first decades of the twentieth century were trying to establish the nature of English as a school subject, they were also trying to establish a professional identity. Audio-visual equipment played only a minor role in each of those endeavors, yet examining the introduction and appropriation of technology in classrooms offers the opportunity to scrutinize, in limited though informative ways, how teachers saw themselves, their students, and the work of teaching writing.

EQUIPMENT FOR TEACHING PROFESSIONALS

The Committee of Ten provided a concise definition of the purposes of English: "(1) to enable the pupil to understand the expressed thoughts of others and to give expression to thoughts of his own; and (2) to cultivate a taste for reading, to give the pupil some acquaintance with good literature, and to furnish him with the means of extending that acquaintance" (*Report of the Committee of Ten* 86). The committee did not describe in useful detail what should be taught or how best to teach it, and both are, of course, the primary daily exigencies of class-room teachers. When the Committee released its report in 1893, they counted 202,963 high school students, which represented less than one percent of the total population of the country (Krug 1:11). At the turn of the century, only 11% of those attending high school graduated, and a "school year" might mean as few as eighty-six meetings (Cuban, *How Teachers Taught* 31). By 1918, and for reasons not entirely informed by a deep conviction that all students could learn (for example, fear of youth crime), every state passed compulsory school attendance laws (Urban and Wagoner 163). The number of public high school students grew to 2,200,389 by 1920; by 1930, it was 4,399,422 (Krug 2: 42). College enrollment also increased during these years, but did not keep pace with the explosive growth in high schools. Moreover, the majority of those enrolling in high school did not have the intention or the wherewithal to attend college. The willingness of some secondary school English teachers to utilize audio-visual equipment was driven partly by the classroom and curricular conditions that arose during this period of rapid expansion: under-prepared and disengaged students, vocational mandates, and the mission to inculcate an appreciation for literature.

To address the increased enrollment in public schools, states instituted significant changes in teacher preparation and certification. At the turn of the twentieth century, no state required high school graduation or professional training for teacher certification. Teacher certification, where required, was granted through examination. One survey reports, however, that in 1905 about 70% of male and 53% of female teachers were college graduates (Krug 1: 187). Within a quarter century, twenty-one states required both professional training and at least a high school diploma for teacher certification (Tyack 419). With the concomitant growth in departments and schools of education, teaching was professionalized, and its professional status encouraged classroom teachers to conceptualize their work in new ways. A survey of English teacher preparation published in 1927 notes that "English teachers are prone to complain that administrators think anyone can teach English and that they employ as English teachers those who have no general preparation in English" (Jewett 178), suggesting that it didn't take long for English teachers to recognize and assert that there were indeed specific skills and training necessary to successfully teach their subject.

An aspect of establishing a professional identity includes determining and claiming what is necessary to do one's work, and high school teachers' appropriation of emerging audio-visual technologies reflected their move toward a fuller professional identity. Both critics and reformers of public education in the early decades of the twentieth century conducted studies of the costs and expenses associated with teaching the various school subjects. When undertaken by critics, such studies sought to root out inefficiency. When undertaken on behalf of English teachers, the ensuing reports conclude that English teachers had greater student loads than other teachers, and the costs of English teaching were modest when compared to other subjects, particularly science. Books, pens, and paper accounted for the largest expenditures for English teaching. Those reports often call for increased funding for English materials, which can be seen as an important early gesture to establish a professional identity by complementing specialized training with specialized equipment. For example, NCTE's report from its Committee on Equipment for School and College Work, published in 1913, recommends that each "English teacher should have, at least upon occasion, the use of a room equipped with a lantern and a reflectoscope and a good supply of slides and pictures for projection. In small schools where a lantern is impossible, the need may be met in part by means of sets of pictures" (Butler, et al. 183).

Mary Crawford's "The Laboratory Equipment of the Teacher of English," published in 1915, is more emphatic: "One of the advances made of late years in the teaching of English is the demand for departmental equipment other than the instructor's training or library facilities" (145). The association with scientific apparatus is deliberate, and she declares that despite the English teacher's expanding knowledge of English as a subject matter, "his equipment has, until recently, remained as it was decades ago" (145). Crawford identifies an array of equipment that "may help to bring the teaching of English to its own": maps and charts; reference books; early slide projectors known as projection lanterns; handheld slide viewers such as stereographs, stereopticons and reflectoscopes; prints, postcards, and pictures; and the phonograph (145). William Hawley Davis, a high school English teacher in Maine, calls upon his colleagues to ask for more than "the minimum equipment" of paper and ink in "The Teaching of English Composition":

> Is there in our field nothing corresponding to the wireless apparatus which is so vitalizing the teaching of electricity, the surveying instrument and the slide rule which are provided for the teacher of geometry and logarithms, the visits to factories and legislatures, to historical and artistic collections, with which our colleagues make significant their instruction in history, economics, and the classics? (291–92)

AUDIO-VISUAL AIDS IN THE CLASSROOM

It's not possible to know how extensively audio-visual aids were adopted during the first decades of the twentieth century, but a 1918 survey of Ohio high schools reports the following results: nineteen of thirty respondents indicated their schools had a "Victrola and educational records"; twenty-one of thirty respondents indicated they had a stereoptican and slides; and twenty-five of twenty-nine respondents affirmed they used pictures in teaching English (McCrosky 114). The survey report concludes with a statement articulating fundamental goals of English instruction that don't overturn those offered by the Committee of Ten so much as expand and redirect their emphases: "To develop individuality and self-expression; to vitalize the student's contact with the world; To develop literary rather than analytic study; to develop appreciation of tone and atmosphere; To secure theme material from experience and observation" (McCrosky 117).

Larry Cuban, in *How Teachers Taught*, notes that photographs of classrooms from that time "show rows of bolted-down desks; in some newly built schools rooms were set aside for 'recitation'; and master schedules typically allotted the major portion of time to teachers' asking questions of students" (32). Romiett Stevens conducted a Teachers College study published in 1912, *The Question as a Measure of Efficiency in Instruction*, and used both a stopwatch and stenographer to observe one hundred high school teachers teaching various subjects. She calculated that students faced an average of 395 questions per day by their teachers. Almost a third of the teachers she observed were firing upward of two hundred questions per period at students, a practice she labels "the pace that kills" (17). Teacher-talk accounted for 64% of classroom discourse, and most of the student-talk consisted of only short sentences or one-word responses.

Some English teachers who embraced audio-visual aids certainly did so, in part, to fulfill a pedagogical desire to move from an exclusively teacher-centered classroom to a more student-centered classroom. Audio-visual aids offered such teachers opportunities to turn from recitation to student involvement—though student involvement was often restricted to passing around postcards or taking turns with a stereopticon. Nevertheless, there was a growing sense among some educators that the pupil was not meant to fit the school but that the school should be made to fit the pupil. A report released in 1918 by the National Education Association, "The Cardinal Principles of Education," proposes ideals for schooling that emphasize student development within social accommodation, a striking departure from the recommendations of the Committee of Ten. Some teachers began to see their role as providing their students with social experiences that many in the surge of incoming students were deprived because of their socioeconomic backgrounds. In "The Relation of Moving Pictures to English Composition," a presentation delivered at the New England Association of Teachers of English in 1914, Carolyn M. Gerrish of Boston's Girls Latin School asks: "How can the teacher of English composition utilize this great instrument for cultural ends?" (226). Gerrish is particularly keen on the vicarious experiences and perspectives motion pictures offer teachers of "the mass of students [. . .] whose horizon is bounded by the city street, whose experience of life is narrowed to the maintenance of a sordid existence in a squalid tenement district," which she contrasts with "the fortunate few who teach in schools in well-to-do residential districts where pupils come from homes pervaded by the atmosphere of culture and the doing of things that count in community life" (226). She suggests schools acquire "moving-picture paraphernalia" for their students' enrichment and predicts they will "become a valuable adjunct in the mastery of skill in English composition" (230). The first catalogue of motion pictures available for schools to rent actually appeared in 1910 and listed over a thousand titles in its 336 pages (Saettler, *History*98). Gerrish's approach to English composition, though, is entirely occupied by writing about literary texts, the most pervasive approach described by teachers of that time as they endeavored to find ways of using audio-visual aids in writing instruction. Audio-visual aids were vaunted as a means of capturing student attention, showing them sights they'd never see, and providing them images from books they showed little interested in.

Others who enthusiastically endorsed the benefits of using movies in English classrooms, however, did so as a means of cultivating "proper taste" in movies for similar reasons often offered for requiring students to read literary classics. In "Defining the Cinema Problem," published in 1932, William Lewin defines the cinema problem as follows: movie producers need to recoup their investments; to do so they need to "please the masses"; the masses have poor taste and regrettably prefer the low-brow to the high-minded. He describes a study conducted in several high schools that compared students' taste in movies with that of professional critics. The results of the study indicated that the taste of high school seniors "resembled" that of the critics, while the taste of younger students did not. Offering students "guidance" in their movie selection, he argues, is therefore essential. Furthermore, Lewin contends that the best solution to the cinema problem might be a committee of English teachers who preview movies before their release to rate their "artistic excellence": "Let us therefore have some common consent as to the nature of this problem. Escape it we cannot. We must face it constructively and determine where progress lies" (388). Proposing that movie producers allow English teachers to pass judgment on their films before release seems now a quaint overestimation of the emergent profession's importance. By 1935, the editors of *The English Journal* would declare that the "first chapters in the probably long history of the teaching of photoplay appreciation in American schools are now complete" (Davis, "Editorial" 241). Indeed, the editorial asserts that the primary aim of "photoplay appreciation" is "profoundly influencing pupils' taste" (241).

In ways that parallel current conditions, the classroom English teacher of a century ago wrestled with claiming and controlling technology, for then, as now, teachers not only appropriate––but sometimes feel appropriated by––technology. Robert W. Neal begins his 1917 article in *The English Journal*, "Making the Devil Useful," by assuring colleagues that "the moving picture is not an invention of the devil"; movies are "here to stay, and we shall have to make the best of them" (658). Similarly, a quarter century later, the introduction to the collection *Radio and English Teaching: Experiences, Problems, and Procedures* notes sympathetically: "As they glance around them at our dubious millennium of machinery, thoughtful teachers no doubt often feel that teaching can be mechanical enough, unfortunately, without machines as an accomplice" (Herzberg 1).

What often occurs when teachers defensively appropriate new technologies, however, is that they minimize many of the creative possibilities of those technologies by using them primarily as additions to existing, conservative teaching practices and curricula. Neal argues, for example, that the "photo-play" can help teachers reach students in ways not previously available, but his recommendations for using the photoplay are exclusively directed toward the study of literature: "To this end, the turning into scenario form the scenes from the books read will greatly help, it being understood that the pupil's 'script' of the scene shall be very full, representing all the 'business' in detail" (659). Variations of this approach characterize many of the pedagogical recommendations in the professional literature of the time regarding the use of audio-visual equipment. Teachers were encouraged, for example, to have students describe in detail the characters from literature depicted on penny postcards.

The term, or concept of, "concreteness" appears throughout early descriptions of the virtues of audio-visual aids in English teaching, and it is valorized and set against "verbalism." Mary Crawford declares in 1915: "All education is tending more and more toward concreteness" (147). In *The Evolution of American Educational Technology*, Paul Saettler maintains that the impulse to cast emergent educational hardware in nonverbal roles, and traditional media such as lectures and textbooks in verbal roles, was particularly common in the first half of the twentieth century. Educators who did so "justified the use of visual materials to combat verbalism in the instructional process" and were often "preoccupied with the effects of devices and procedures rather than with the differences in individual learners or the selection or design of instructional content" (8). In other words, teachers often used audio-visual aids to act upon, rather than interact with, students. While the move away from "verbalism" may be commendable, the "concreteness" audio-visual aids offered was deemed a more dynamic delivery system for transmitting the cultural values and literary interpretations they wanted to instill in their students. For example, Neal claims that "pictured action can be made a means of developing the internal picturing power of the pupil. In other words, it can be used to get him in the habit of picturing in his mind the action of which he reads" (659). Crawford calls for more extensive "laboratory equipment" not only as means toward greater professional standing for English teachers but also because such aids "deepen the impression made by reading" and "may stimulate a sluggish imagination" (148). The stereopticon and reflectoscope (and pictures and postcards) excited many English teachers primarily because they provided students vivid representations of locales, characters, and scenes from literature.

NEW TECHNOLOGY FOR COMPOSITION

High school English teachers in the early decades of the last century had little preparation for the teaching of writing. Ida A. Jewett's 1927 study, *English in State Teachers Colleges*, indicates that courses in the teaching of composition were not common in the seventy-one four-year white state teacher colleges then in existence. Only eleven offered a course in methods of instruction in composition, while over half offered courses in "Dramatics and Play Production" (19). Moreover, Jewett identified an important distinction that still marks some secondary school English teacher education: "The small number of courses in creative writing, versification, and the like, as compared with the number in literature, indicates that the English departments are distinguishing between the values of production and accomplishment and those in consumption and utilization" (131). Jewett's distinction between textual production and consumption is a useful one, for as suggested above, early use of audio-visual aids was more often used as a means of aiding consumption rather than production.

The writing instruction most students received in the schools during the first decades of the twentieth century was conscribed by emphases on spelling and correctness through drills and the writing of short "themes." English teachers typically considered their subject as comprised of three parts: grammar, literature, and composition, and composition was often divided evenly between written and oral composition. There were efforts and arguments, however, to reconfigure writing instruction. "English Problems after the War," an address delivered in 1918 to English teachers in Utica, New York by Syracuse

University's Horace Ainsworth Eaton, is representative of such arguments. After declaring the war won—"marvelously and completely won" (308)—he declares that the teaching of composition, even more than the teaching of literature, demands "work in the new spirit" (311): "Teachers will concern themselves more with ideas than with the meticulous details of form. Ideas come first, ideas expressively and effectively phrased; impeccable spelling and faultless grammar are sorry substitutes. We are training children to be citizens of a great society, in which ideas and ideals are to have supreme social force" (312). The 1919 report of the Subcommittee on Composition and Rhetoric, part of NCTE's Committee on Economy of Time in English, begins by asserting that the "value of rhetoric teaching depends on pupils' ability to use what they have learned" and offers "recommendations in terms of attainments rather than knowledge" (Miles, et al. 554). They recognized that composition is less a body of facts than a practice. The subcommittee encouraged a new attitude to teach students to "look upon all rhetorical principles and devices as means which, having proved helpful to others in accomplishing purposes through language, will probably help them also" (555). Furthermore, "They should think of rhetoric not as rhetoric but as a means of gaining their own ends, quite as effective outside as within the classroom" (555). The subcommittee even asserts: "No student ought to be required to produce a composition unless there is some reason for doing it over and above the command or request of the teacher" (564). The report criticizes secondary school teachers who "instead of using their college courses as a background [. . .] are inclined to reproduce them" (568).

To be sure, there were teachers who urged the incorporation of new technology in English classes so students could produce original writing. There were teaching suggestions to have students compose radio reports for imaginary delivery or travelogues to accompany slide projections. Hardy Finch, a member of NCTE's Committee on Standards for Motion Pictures and Newspapers, reports in 1939 that more than two hundred secondary schools produced films, and he predicts that soon "practically every school in the country will be making or will have made its own film offering" ("Film Production" 365). A year later he reports the existence of over three thousand photoplay clubs ("Motion Picture" 466). Perhaps not surprisingly, many of the films made in the schools were dramatizations of literature, and the production of such films was intended to develop students' careful reading of literary texts. Student- or school-made films, however, were not restricted to such productions. Finch also cites examples of students filming historical reenactments, filmed versions of student writing, and school-produced newsreels and safety films. Finch lists the opportunity for student writing among the most important purposes for high school student movie making.

William Hawley Davis's "The Teaching of English Composition: Its Present State," published in 1917, calls for teachers to ask for classroom equipment that included a stereopticon with a projector and screen, a phonograph with educational records—and a duplicating machine. He recommends the duplicating machine be used "to bring typical errors and defects—drawn, not from some strange and remote list in a textbook where they are necessarily mingled with much that is not typical, but from the pulsating product of a known fellow student" (292). Even more importantly, the machine should be used to display "good composition work where it will secure the only real reward ever given to good composition work—that of being *read*" (292). Davis even proposes English classrooms should have a "printing outfit" that would allow students to write for wider audiences while benefiting from the proofreading necessary when typesetting. Students could produce fliers, announcements, and even a monthly magazine. He concludes: "In instituting these improvements it will at once become apparent that the equipment of the English composition department may easily be too meager, that particularly in dealing with a subject not reducible to a tangible unit the pedagogical devices recommended by commonsense should not be neglected" (294).

Not every teacher of a century ago received, or requested, a stereopticon or phonograph, and many no doubt bristled at the association of English classrooms with laboratories. Nevertheless, the use of audio-visual aids concurred with the emergence of secondary school English. Their classroom uses highlight significant movements within high school English, movements that manifested a curricular push-pull away and toward college English. Secondary school English teachers often claimed audio-visual equipment to indicate a new professionalism, yet descriptions of its uses reveal that innovative technology was more often used in retrograde ways. As high school English teachers struggled to legitimize the subject of English and struggled to accommodate an expanding student population less interested in, or served by, the traditional English curricula established by their college preparatory forebears, they often turned to new technology as a means of enhancing the delivery of curricula. Yet what was often delivered was a mostly traditional—and enduring—view of teachers, students, and English.

Works Cited

Butler, William M., et al. "English Equipment." *The English Journal* 2.3 (1913): 178–84. Print.

Coulter, Vincil Carey. "Financial Support of English Teaching." *The English Journal* 1.1 (1912): 24–29. Print.

Crawford, Mary. "The Laboratory Equipment of the Teacher of English." *The English Journal* 4.3 (1915): 145–51. Print.

Cuban, Larry. *How Teachers Taught: Constancy and Change in American Classrooms, 1890–1990.* 2nd ed. New York: Teachers College, 1993. Print.

Davis, William Hawley. "The Teaching of English Composition: Its Present State." *The English Journal* 6.5 (1917): 285–94. Print.

—"Editorial: How Much Analysis of Photoplays?" *The English Journal* 24.3 (1935): 241–42. Print.

Eaton, Horace Ainsworth. "English Problems After the War." *The English Journal* 8.5 (1919): 308–312. Print.

Finch, Hardy. "Film Production in the School—A Survey." *The English Journal* 28.5 (1939): 365–71. Print.

—. "Motion Picture Activities in the High School." *The English Journal* 29.6 (1940): 465–70. Print.

Gerrish, Carolyn M. "The Relation of Moving Pictures to English Composition." *The English Journal* 4.4 (1915): 226–30. Print.

Herzberg, Max J. "Introduction: The English Classroom in this Listening Age." *Radio and English Teaching: Experiences, Problems, and Procedures.* Ed. Max J. Herzberg. New York: D. Appleton-Century, 1941. 1–16. Print.

Jewett, Ida A. *English in State Teachers Colleges: A Catalogue Study.* New York: Teachers College, 1927. Print.

Krug, Edward A. *The Shaping of the American High School.* 2 vols. New York: Harper & Row, 1964–1972. Print.

Lewin, William. "Defining the Cinema Problem." *The English Journal* 21.5 (1932): 385–88. Print.

McCrosky, Cecile B. "The Administration of English in the High-School Curriculum." *The English Journal* 7.2 (1918): 108–17. Print.

Miles, William Dudley, et al. "The Economy of Time in English." *The English Journal* 8.9 (1918): 554–568. Print.

Neal, Robert W. "Making the Devil Useful." *The English Journal* 2.10 (1913): 658–60. Print.

Report of the Committee of Ten on Secondary School Studies: With the Reports of the Conferences Arranged by the Committee. New York: American Book Company, 1894. Print.

Saettler, Paul. *A History of Instructional Technology.* New York: McGraw-Hill, 1968. Print.

—. *The Evolution of American Educational Technology.* Greenwich, CT: Information Age Publishing, 2004. Print.

Stevens, Romiett. *The Question as a Measure of Efficiency in Instruction.* New York: Teachers College, 1912. Print.

Tyack, David B., ed. *Turning Points in American Educational History.* Waltham, MA: Blaisdell, 1967. Print.

Urban, Wayne, and Jennings Wagoner, Jr. *American Education: A History.* New York: McGraw-Hill, 1996. Print.

7 Textbooks and Their Pedagogical Influences in Higher Education: A Bibliographic Essay

Sherry Rankins Robertson and Duane Roen

> *Without textbooks there would have been almost no vehicles for developing ideas about writing and learning [specifically to early 1900s] to write, and without student essays [embedded in these books] there would be almost no evidence of exactly what went on in the composition courses where the theories were used.*
>
> —Robert Connors

Other than the instructor, textbooks have always been the primary source of technology that has provided authority in the writing classroom. From a Vygotskian perspective, a textbook is one of many tools mediating human psychological processes and human interaction. Textbooks include language that facilitates the communication of the values and practices of discourse communities, of whole cultures. Further, as Thomas Kuhn suggests, textbooks are the "pedagogic vehicles for the perpetuation of normal science" (137) rather than revolutionary thinking. As such, they often encapsulate the standard wisdom of the day. The discipline of rhetoric and composition has used textbooks as an historical lens to retrospectively construct a theoretical overview of norms for any given time period.

THE CLASSICAL PERIOD, *CIRCA* 460 BCE–410 CE

Greek universities developed from the philosophical and rhetorical schools. For example, as Francesco Cordasco notes, the University of

Athens grew out of three of these schools—the Stoic, the Peripatetic school of Aristotle, and the Academy (9). In higher education in Greece, especially in Athens, speaking instruction was more valued than writing instruction, but both were informed by rhetoric (Marrou; Welch).

Among the works treated as textbooks of the period, the *Dissoi Logoi* (literally translated as "different words") shows the influence of such fifth-century BCE thinkers as Hippias, Gorgias, Protagoras, and Socrates (McComiskey). Composed *circa* 400 BCE, the *Dissoi Logoi* (Robinson) examines multiple perspectives of topics that were popular in philosophy and rhetoric at the time—democracy, ethics, epistemology, education, memory, and the art of discourse. The eighth of the nine sections in the *Dissoi Logoi* focuses on the art of discourse (*logon techne*), advocating that rhetors should be able to argue both sides of an issue succinctly.

Some rhetorical treatises of the classical period have stood the test of time. Aristotle's *Rhetoric*, compiled from his students' lecture notes between 367–347 and 335–323 BCE, focuses on "the faculty of observing in any given case the available means of persuasion" (24).

In the first century BCE in Rome, the well-known politician Marcus Tullisu Cicero wrote prolifically on rhetoric, but *De Inventione* (84 BCE) and *De Oratore* (55 BCE) are considered especially influential. *De Inventione,* as the title suggests, focuses heavily on invention. *De Oratore* is Cicero's most comprehensive treatment of rhetoric. A century later in Rome, Marcus Fabius Quintilianus—Quintilian—authored *Institutio Oratoria* (*Education of the Orator*), the most extensive rhetorical treatise that survives from the classical period. In the twelve books of *Institutio Oratoria,* Quintilian explains views on invention, arrangement, style, memory, and delivery.

THE MEDIEVAL PERIOD, *CIRCA* 410–1300 CE

According to R. Freedman Butts, Medieval textbooks are a rich source of information about education of the era, especially about the liberal arts. From these textbooks, "We know what they expected of students, namely, the mastery of the textbooks" (194).

As noted by George A. Kennedy, the Medieval era of rhetoric can be divided into three distinct periods, and different rhetorical perspectives reigned in each: Classical rhetoric thrived in the monastic schools during the early Medieval period (the fifth through the eighth centuries CE); Ciceronian rhetoric and the liberal arts dominated from the ninth through the twelfth centuries; rhetoric focused on practical needs in the late Medieval period (the thirteenth and fourteenth centuries). As Butts notes, while academics readily accepted Aristotle's work in the humanities (too readily in the minds of some educators of the time), his work in science was slower to gain acceptance because it was deemed inconsistent with church doctrine (Butts 187).

As noted by Cordasco, Martianus Capella's *The Marriage of Philology and Mercury*, a popular textbook during the first half of the Middle Ages, includes the seven liberal arts—the quadrivium (arithmetic, geometry, astronomy, and music) and the trivium (grammar, rhetoric, and dialectic). The trivium was defined primarily by classical rhetoricians as well as teachers of antiquity. As noted by Frank Pierrepont Graves, students frequently studied not only textbooks but also functional texts such as forms, legal documents, and letters. As a result, teachers routinely used models to shape students' speaking and writing.

Because the state and the church needed functional communication, the Middle Ages saw the emergence of three common forms of writing: letter writing (*ars dictaminis*), preaching (*ars praedicandi*), and poetics (*ars poetriae*) (Camargo; Morgan; Murphy). Teachers of the day focused first on style (*elocutio*), then arrangement (*dispositio*), and finally invention (*inventio*) (Woods). As Graves notes, pedagogy commonly included memorization, question-and-answer, lecture, and dictation. Also, as Kennedy notes, the *Progymnasmata* (Libanius) remained a popular textbook in the Middle Ages.

THE RENAISSANCE, *CIRCA* 1300–1700 CE

Johannes Gutenberg's invention of the printing press in 1440 represented a major technological advancement that affected the use of textbooks in teaching, including the teaching of writing. Thanks to the printing press, hundreds of rhetorical treatises were published during the Renaissance, but some Classical and Medieval texts were also influential. For instance, the works of Cicero (*De Inventione, On Oratory and Orators*), Tacitus (*Dialogus de Oratoribus*), and Quintilian (*Institutio Oratoria*) were widely used during the Renaissance.

Classical rhetoricians also influenced some textbooks written during the Renaissance. For instance, as Wilbur Samuel Howell notes, Cicero's influence is readily apparent in Richard Sherry's *A Treatise of Schemes and Tropes*, Leonard Cox's *The Art of Crafte of Rhethoryke*, Thomas Wilson's *The Arte of Rhetorique*, and John Ludham's *The Practise of Preaching*—texts of the mid-sixteenth century. Other traditional textbooks of the Renaissance included Lorenze Ruglielmo Traversagni's *Nova Rhetorica*, Stephen Hawes's *Pastime of Pleasure* (an allegorical poem featuring Dame Rethoryke), and William Caxton's *Mirrour of the World* (a translation of a French text of the seven arts and sciences).

The Renaissance also saw a flurry of texts that focused on the rhetoric of style: John Jewel's *Oratio contra Rhetoricam* (*Oration Against Rhetoric*) (see Hudson), Henry Peacham's *The Garden of Eloquence Conteyning the Figures of Grammer and Rhetorick*, Richard Sherry's *Treatise of the Figures of Grammar and Rhetoric*, Richard Rainolde's *The Foundacion of Rhetorike* (a version of the progymnasmata), and Desiderius Erasmus's *Copia: Foundations of the Abundant Style*.

One of the more influential thinkers of the day, Pierre de la Ramee (usually called Peter Ramus) wrote attacks on several classical rhetoricians. In *Arguments in Rhetoric Against Quintilian*, Ramus argues that orators need not be good people. Ramus also attacks Cicero in *Brutinae Quaestiones*. In *Dialectique*, Ramus devotes many pages to arranging ideas.

In addition to influencing his fellow French rhetoricians and logicians, Ramus also had influence across the English Channel. Among the earliest Ramists in England was Gabriel Harvey, who wrote *Ciceronianus* and *Rhetor*. At about the same time, Dudley Fenner wrote *The Artes of Logike and Rethorike*, which emphasizes elocution and pronunciation.

THE EIGHTEENTH CENTURY

In the English-speaking world Hugh Blair's *Lectures on Rhetoric and Belles Lettres* and George Campbell's *The Philosophy of Rhetoric* were immensely popular in the later eighteenth century and into the nineteenth century, and both were used as university textbooks. Blair's book, reprinted nearly two dozen times during those centuries, emphasizes moral improvement, reason, and taste. While rhetoric appeals to reason and emotions, belles lettres focuses on aesthetically pleasing works. Both rhetoric and belles lettres rely on refined taste. For Blair the effective rhetor has good character, knowledge of the subject, industriousness, good models, practice, and rhetorical theory. Campbell's book, a study of human nature, includes treatment of imaginative literature, elocution, and a canon for both speakers and writers.

Although better known as an economist, Adam Smith was also an influential rhetorician, as evidenced by the publication of his *Lectures on Rhetoric and Belle Lettres*. Smith's lectures emphasize communication and forms of composition, including taxonomies of a wide range of texts in fields such as science, history, and poetry.

As noted by Winifred Bryan Horner, among other influential texts of the eighteenth century was Thomas Sheridan's *Course of Lectures on Elocution*, based on lectures he delivered from 1756 to 1762. Others included Thomas Gibbons's *Rhetoric*, John Holmes's *The Art of Rhetoric Made Easy*, John Mason's *An Essay on Elocution or Pronunciation*, Joseph Priestley's *A Course on Oratory and Criticism*, John Ward's *A System of Oratory*, and John Walker's *Elements of Elocution*.

THE NINETEENTH CENTURY

During the nineteenth century, textbook publishing became a business, and there was an increase in the number of available texts in addition to a wider distribution of the texts (Carr, Carr, and Schultz). Textbooks took on a new role for a variety of reasons, including the demand for different types of texts, and textbooks were used for training not only students but also teachers (Roen, Goggin, and Clary-Lemon). Many of the texts produced were a reflection of the culture and value system of the time, but "composition books are commonly compiled by a single author [. . .] offering materials 'borrowed' from earlier books" (Carr, Carr, and Schultz 12). Two events during the nineteenth century that catapulted composition textbooks were an increase of college enrollment due to the end of the Civil War and the establishment of rhetoric and composition programs in American universities.

Two eighteenth century British written texts dominated nineteenth century rhetorical instruction. *Philosophy of Rhetoric* by George Campbell treated rhetoric like a science; Hugh Blair in *Lectures on Rhetoric and Belles-Lettres* treats rhetoric as an art, and focuses on stylistic features. Robert Connors notes that a consequence of the belletristic emphasis on the individual was texts that focused on students' personal experiences and feelings. Richard Whately's *Elements of Rhetoric*, written in 1828, focuses on "'argumentative composition,'" which discusses "various logical processes and topics" (Carr, Carr, and Schultz 52).

The first American authored text was John Witherspoon's *Lectures on Moral Philosophy and Eloquence*, which covers topics of origins and structures of language. Alexander Jamieson, a textbook writer, but not a teacher or theorist of rhetoric, produced *A Grammar of Rhetoric and Polite Literature* in 1818, which includes remnants of Campbell's work. A text that promotes application with "self-contained exercises to demonstrate the principles" is Samuel Newman's *A Practical System of Rhetoric* written in 1834 (Carr, Carr, and Schultz 58). *Elements of the Art of Rhetoric* by Henry Noble Day focuses on development of ideas and arrangement; his text explores "possible processes for development" in depth to "be understood in terms of enlightening the understanding, pleasing the imagination, moving the passions, and influencing the will" (Johnson 69). This 1866 text sets the stage for what later becomes the modes of discourse.

Three texts that pushed into the twentieth century that were published and had a "practical" influence on composition, as a discipline, in the nineteenth century were Barrett Wendell's 1876 *Foundations of Rhetoric*, John Genung's 1886 *Practical Elements of Rhetoric*, and Adam Sherman Hill's 1895 *The Principles of Rhetoric and Their Application*. According to Connors in "Textbooks and the Evolution of the Discipline," these three men were "genuine rhetoricians" who "invented out of the whole cloth of personal observation, supposition, and selective plagiarism." Connors attributes the current-traditional model, patterns of exposition and modes of discourse, and the development of composition in America to the textbooks of Hill, Wendell, and Genung (186–187). Sharon Crowley discusses these three texts as "self-reflexivity," with an additional text, Fred Newton Scott and Joseph V. Denney's *Paragraph-Writing*, to balance out what she calls "the big four" during the 1890s (*Methodical Memory* 141).

According to James Berlin in "The Growth of the Discipline: 1900–1920" in *Rhetoric and Reality*, Adam Sherman Hill's text *Principles of Rhetoric* is "[. . .] divided into two parts, the first dealing with superficial correctness and the second with the forms of discourse. Students wrote a theme for each class day—a total of six per week—

using uniform theme paper" (37). It includes correction aid for "spelling, punctuation, usage, syntax" and students were often asked to rewrite to "correct their errors" (Berlin 38). In addition to the daily themes, students "wrote 'longer fortnightly themes' that consisted of six expository themes in the first semester and two themes in each of the other [description, argument, or narration] forms in the second [semester]" (Berlin 38). In addition to this writing, students were required to read English literature, hold conferences with teachers, and take exams. Herbert Creek, who was a student at DePauw University in 1896, writes in his article "Forty Years of Composition Teaching" about his encounters with Hill's text. Creek describes Hill's text as "The Mistakes of Great Authors," and writes that the text dissected the work of famous writers to point out the errors. Creek says, "[W]e wrote no papers in which the instructor would mark our mistakes" (4). Creek counters with his description of Barrett Wendell's *Principles of Rhetoric (1876)*, a text that teaches one how to write clearly beginning with a topic sentence that encourages logical paragraphs that summarize and use leading ideas (5). In *English Composition*, Wendell illustrates that writing is a means of collecting and organizing ideas. He (with Quackenbos) promotes the use of a journal for thought keeping (Crowley, "Invention in Nineteenth-Century Rhetoric" 54). Much of what is still valued about writing in the twenty-first century seems to come from Wendell. Wendell can be seen as "a grandfather" of modern rhetoric because his text focuses on means of invention rather than what was being privileged at the time [a focus on grammar].

Genung's *Practical Elements of Rhetoric* pays particular attention to steps of invention: "six stages that grew out of the basic three" (Crowley, *Methodical Memory* 77). Genung incorporates the modes of discourse (narration, exposition, argumentation, description, and persuasion) in this text (118). Still today what was once intended as simple strategies for invention [modes] is still influencing first-year writing curricula.

The Twentieth Century

In Bruce Ballenger's 2007 CCCC presentation on textbooks, he cites Connors's work as indicating the following central ideas that were evident in texts during each of the indicated time periods:

> **1900–1915:** Style and rhetoric, borrowed from oral tradition.

1915–1945: Developmental approach that began with word, then sentence, then paragraph, then whole composition.

1945–1970: "Thesis" rhetoric that is organized around one "master idea."

Berlin acknowledges Charles Baldwin's 1902 text *College Manual of Rhetoric* as an "authority on ancient rhetoric" (42). According to A. M. Tibbetts's "'Argument' in Nineteenth Century American Rhetoric Textbooks," Baldwin uses Aristotle's kinds of persuasion in this text (237). Tibbetts quotes Baldwin from his text, *College Manual of Rhetoric*, as saying, "argument is not something distinct from persuasion, it is a part of persuasion" (238). Baldwin seems to be one of the first rhetoricians [since Whatley] to reinforce Aristotle's concepts. Tibbetts observes that Baldwin was probably the most knowledgeable about the history and values of classical rhetoric of his time. Berlin adds that Baldwin's text pushes for ability to "use language logically" through persuasion, exposition, and argumentation of speaking and writing (42).

In his 1907 review of Carpenter's *Rhetoric and English Composition*, Isaac Choate states the text focuses too much on the "right" way to correct errors (401). Another text that focuses on the "rules of writing" in the early twentieth century is Edwin Campbell Woolley's *Handbook of Composition*. This was the first handbook, which consisted of "exactly 350 rules," In the preface Woolley identifies the audience as:

> students of composition for reference, at the direction of the instructor, in case of errors in themes. Second it may be used for independent reference by persons who have writing of any kind to do [. . .] on matters of good usage, grammar, spelling, punctuation, paragraphing, manuscript-arrangement, or letter-writing. (359)

In Creek's discussion of *Handbook of Composition* he coins this text as "one of the most successful texts ever published" (6). Creek describes *Handbook of Composition* as a practice for teachers to use the numerated rules to simply make a numeric indicator on a student's paper as a reference point for the student to locate and learn from the error; while the materials read as though teachers are a primary audience for Woolley's text, Creek indicates that this text was written for "farm boys [who] were coming to the state universities" (6). Berlin writes that

Woolley's *Handbook of Composition* was "used to get rid of 'illiteracy'" (41). This text is critical as it promotes a focus on correctness, resulting in teacher workload to include error marking with corresponding grammar numbers from the text on students' work.

Introduced during the nineteenth century and referred to as "class books" or "instructors," readers brought the opportunity to analyze texts and served as "storage for cultural materials" (Carr, Carr, and Schultz). Lane Cooper's 1907 *Theories of Style* is a reader with a mixture of "heavily romantic theory of literary composition" (374). The table of contents ranges from Aristotle and Plato to Coleridge and Thoreau. Cooper includes a variety of pieces on style, including Voltaire, Schopenhauer, and Pater. Cooper closes the text with two pieces on prose. Frances Campbell Berkeley's reader, *A College Course in Writing from Models*, provides the "models" that were being offered in the sophomore English classes. Additionally, Berkeley includes material from editorials, criticisms, and point of view. In the introductory materials Berkeley appeals to the reader that the text would rarely change the included materials and this text was intended to answer the "practical question—'What must I do to improve my writing?'" (384).

Representative Essays in Modern Thought, written by Harrison Ross Steeves and Frank Humphrey Ristine in 1913, is a reader filled with essays from education, history, and philosophy. Creek commented that this text was a "sensation among young teachers" (7). The idea behind this text is that it would expose students to materials that were complex and needed to be critically read—this would teach students to "think clearly and therefore write clearly" (7). Norman Foerster, Frederick Manchester, and Karl Young's readers *Essays for College Men* (1913) and *Essays for College Men, Second Series* (1915) include readings that respond to timely theoretical questions for young men, such as "What is a College For?"; "The Social Value of The College-Bred"; "Inaugural Address" ; "The Moral Equivalent of War" (390–92). Maurice Fulton's 1912 *Expository Writing* focuses on an advanced level writing course during the sophomore or junior year; it was intended for "imitation and analysis" through the use of study questions (393).

Scott and Denney's *New Composition* was a dominant text at the same time as George Rice Carpenter's *Rhetoric and English Composition* and Baldwin's *College Manual*. These three texts seemed to be "neck-to-neck" in popularity from 1910–1915. Norman Foerster and John Marcellus Steadman's 1914 *Sentences and Thinking: A Practice*

Book in Sentence Making stayed in print from 1914–1951 and was considered by Connors as the "'first modern rhetoric'" (416). Intended for first-year composition, it is set up as a review for "mastery of fundamentals," and includes "essentials" rather than being "comprehensive" as the texts before had done (416). William Strunk's *Elements of Style* focuses on rules of usage and style and includes commonly misspelled words and misused expressions; the text was reprinted in 1935 by Harcourt Brace publishing and again in 1959 when E. B. White, a student of Strunk's, revised it (406).

Creek notes that during the time period of 1915–1945, labeled as "developmental approach that began with word, then sentence, then paragraph, then whole composition," oral themes come to the surface in several texts, but did not stay for long because speech faculty formed their own departments, and college enrollments increased (due to the end of World War I). In 1918 Frank Scott noted that handbooks were "usurping the place of textbooks as rhetoric" (Connors, "Handbooks" 93). [This chapter does not include handbooks on a whole, but selected handbooks that took the place of composition textbooks have been mentioned.] In 1927, twenty-seven midwestern colleges were surveyed and it was found that 85% of composition classrooms were using handbooks and 45% were using handbooks exclusively (no other text in the class) (95). The production of "special textbooks for technical, agricultural, or business students" resulted in the less standard literature and more popular/appropriate/topical articles for composition (Creek 9). Until the 1930s composition was considered to be in the "Dark Ages" due to the lack of journals, which affected the stagnant content of the textbooks and lack of space for discoveries to occur (Connors, "Textbooks" 190).

The sole purpose of *The Writing of English* by John Matthew Manly and Edith Rickert was to "awaken students to the desire of self-expression" (429). This text was used in classes with students, currently known as Basic Writers, who were below the standard. This text was used at the University of Chicago and real changes were seen with the students: 33% of students were able to move on to freshman English, 33% were "permitted to take a supplementary half-course," and 33% were given freshman credit without delay (430). At the same time, *Composition for College Students* by Joseph M. Thomas, Frederick A. Manchester, Franklin W. Scott is praised [in a review by Stanley Swarthy] as "solid, substantial" and Swarthy states that the authors do not talk down to the students; the review indicates that the text has a "new section" titled "presenting an argument," and is criticized for not including more grammar (219).

Edwin Woolley, Franklin Scott, and Frederick Bracher's *College Handbook of Composition* is four hundred pages long, but includes both a rhetoric and handbook in one. While the book was marketed as one that was "liberal," Raymond Howes goes on to say that the idea of the book is "not to teach students to communicate, but 'to get his ideas decently in order on the printed page.'" *College Handbook of Composition* is less "rigid than its predecessor" but ranks as a "satisfactory" handbook among the "old school" (865). *Writing and Thinking* by Foerster and Steadman builds on the idea that paragraphs were "larger repetitions of its smallest element" and when writers bring together strong sentences, paragraphs form, and strong paragraphs develop into essays (Crowley, *Methodical Memory* 132). This book parallels with the organizational structure of focusing the individual parts to develop a coherent whole.

Connors calls James McCrimmon's 1941 *Writing with a Purpose* the "current-traditional warhorse" ("Textbooks" 192). Crowley writes in her text *The Methodical Memory* that the book [*Writing with a Purpose*] is "evidence that the current traditional composition theory is still present" in the writing classroom (93). The text was promoted as one that helped students "choose a subject from their inventory of experience, narrow it to a topic, and state it clearly in a sentence," as well as organize ideas with in-depth outlining information (93). Crowley's text goes on to argue that McCrimmon's "revolutionary idea" of a thesis statement had been done 165 years earlier in Campbell's 1776 *Philosophy of Rhetoric*.

Sheridan Baker states in the preface of her 1950 *The Practical Stylist*, "Nothing here is really new; I am simply describing the natural linguistic facts discovered again and again by the heirs of Aristotle." In Robert Caldwell's review of *The Practical Stylist*, the text is described as "dealing with a basic component of the composition process" (87). The text covers punctuation, thesis formation, paragraph and sentence development, word selection and "contribut[ions] to the overall effect of the essay" (87).

In the 1970s, thesis-centered rhetorical texts were produced that focus around one "master idea," and in the 1980s a shift occurred where texts were "process" oriented. At this time, the rise and stabilization of the discipline of rhetoric and composition allowed multiple theories to coexist, which caused an explosion in the types of texts available from the late twentieth through early twenty-first centuries. Due to movements such as postmodernism and post-structuralism, not only did traditional texts exist but alternative texts also emerged. This expansion in the text types affected the production, distribution, and consumption of texts in the market.

The composition textbook has served as an indispensable tool for educators and students throughout the ages. The opportunity to return to another time and recognize the norms of the rhetorical traditions are made available through the texts that dominated the time. While texts have transformed in shape from scrolls to mass-produced full-color printed books, the content has continued to serve as the pedagogical vehicle for interaction in the composition classroom.

WORKS CITED

Aristotle. *Rhetoric.* Trans. W. Rhys Roberts. *Rhetoric and Poetics of Aristotle.* Ed. Freidrich Solmsen. New York: Modern Library, 1954. (Original work published *ca.* 346 BCE.) Print.

Baldwin, Charles. *College Manual of Rhetoric.* London: Longman's, Green, and Co., 1902. Print.

Ballenger, Bruce. Conference on College Composition and Communication. Hilton Hotel, New York. 22 March 2007. Presentation.

Baker, Sheridan. *The Practical Stylist.* New York: Thomas Y. Crowell Co., 1950. Print.

Berkeley, Francis Campbell. *A College Course in Writing from Models.* Ed. John Brereton. *The Origins of Composition Studies in the American College, 1875–1925.* Pittsburgh, PA: U of Pittsburgh P, 1995. 378–86. Print.

Berlin, James. *Rhetoric and Reality.* Carbondale: Southern Illinois UP, 1987. Print.

Blair, Hugh. *Lectures on Rhetoric and Belles Lettres.* Ed. David Potter. Carbondale: Southern Illinois UP, 1963. (Original work published 1783.) Print.

Butts, R. Freedman. *A Cultural History of Education.* New York: McGraw-Hill Book Company, 1947. Print.

Caldwell, Robert. Review of *The Practical Stylist* by Sheridan Baker. *English Journal* 67.2 (1978): 87–88. Print.

Camargo, Martin. "Between Grammar and Rhetoric: Composition Teaching at Oxford and Bologna in the Late Middle Ages." *Rhetoric and Pedagogy: Its History, Philosophy, and Practice.* Ed. Winifred B. Horner and

Michael Leff. Mahwah, NJ: Lawrence Erlbaum Associates, 1995. 83–94. Print.

Campbell, George. *The Philosophy of Rhetoric.* Ed. David Potter. Carbondale: Southern Illinois UP, 1963. (Original work published 1776.) Print.

Capella, Martianus. *Martianus Capella and the Seven Liberal Arts: The Marriage of Philology and Mercury.* Ed. S. Stahl, R. Johnson, and E. Burge. New York and London: Columbia UP, 1977. (Original work published 429 CE.) Print.

Carpenter, George Rice. *Rhetoric and English Composition.* New York: MacMillian, 1906. Print.

Carr, Jean Ferguson, Stephen Carr, and Lucille Schultz. *Achieves of Instruction: Nineteenth-Century Rhetorics, Readers and Composition Books in the United States.* Carbondale: Southern Illinois UP, 2005. Print.

Caxton, William. *Mirrour of the World.* Ed. Oliver H. Prior. London: Oxford UP, 1966. (Original work published 1481.) Print.

Choate, Isaac. Review of *Rhetoric and English Composition.* By George Carpenter. *School Review* 15.5 (1907): 400–401. Print.

Cicero. *De Inventione, De Optimo Genere, Oratorum, Topica.* Trans. H. M. Hubble. Cambridge, MA: Harvard UP, 1976. (Original work published *ca.* 86 BCE.) Print.

Cicero. *On Oratory and Orators.* Trans. J. S. Watson. Carbondale: Southern Illinois UP, 1986. (Original work published *ca.* 55 BCE.) Print.

Connors, Robert. "Handbooks: History of a Genre." *Rhetoric Society Quarterly* 13.2 (1983): 87–98. Print.

—. Review of *The Origin of Composition Studies in the American College, 1875–1925: A Documentary History* by John Brereton. *Rhetoric Review* 15.2 (1997) 422–425. Print.

—. "Textbooks and the Evolution of the Discipline." *College Composition and Communication* 37.2 (1986): 178–94. Print.

Cooper, Lane. *Theories of Style.* Ed. John Brereton. *The Origins of Composition Studies in the American College, 1875–1925.* Pittsburgh, PA: U of Pittsburgh P, 1995. 373–378.

Cordasco, Francesco. *A Brief History of Education.* Towata, NJ: Littlefield, Adams & Company, 1976. Print.

Cox, Leonard. *The Art of Crafte of Rhethoryke.* Ed. Frederic Ives Carpenter. Chicago, IL: U of Chicago P, 1899. (Original work published 1530.) Print.

Creek, Herbert. "Forty Years of Composition Teaching." *College Composition and Communication* 6.1 (1955): 4–10. Print.

Crowley, Sharon. "Invention in Nineteenth-Century Rhetoric." *College Composition and Communication* 36. 1 (1985): 51–60. Print.

—. *The Methodical Memory: Invention in Current-Traditional Rhetoric.* Carbondale: Southern Illinois UP, 1990. Print.

Day, Henry Noble. *Elements of the Art of Rhetoric*. Hudson, NY: W. Skinner & Co., 1850. Print.

Erasmus, Desiderius. *Collected Works of Erasmus. Literary and Educational Writings 2. De copia / De ratione studii*. Ed. Craig R. Thompson. Toronto: U of Toronto P, 1978. Print.

Fenner, Dudley. *The Artes of Logike and Rethorike. Four Tudor Books on Education*. Ed. Robert D. Pepper. Gainesville, FL: Scholars' Facsimiles and Reprints, 1966. (Original work published 1584.) Print.

Foerster, Norman, Frederick Manchester, and Karl Young. *Essays for College Men*. Ed. John Brereton. *The Origins of Composition Studies in the American College, 1875–1925*. Pittsburgh, PA: U of Pittsburgh P, 1995. 390–391. Print.

—. *Essays for College Men, Second Series*. Ed. John Brereton. *The Origins of Composition Studies in the American College, 1875–1925*. Pittsburgh, PA: U of Pittsburgh P, 1995. 391–92. Print.

Foerster, Norman, and John Marcellus Steadman. "Sentences and Thinking: A Practice Book in Sentence Making." Ed. John Brereton. *The Origins of Composition Studies in the American College, 1875–1925*. Pittsburgh, PA: U of Pittsburgh P, 1995. 415–29. Print.

—. *Writing and Thinking*. Boston, MA: Houghton Mifflin, 1931. Print.

Fulton, Maurice. *Expository Writing*. Ed. John Brereton. *The Origins of Composition Studies in the American College, 1875–1925*. Pittsburgh, PA: U of Pittsburgh P, 1995. 392–406. Print.

Genung, John. *The Practical Elements of Rhetoric*. Boston, MA: Grinn, 1886. Print.

Gibbons, Thomas. *Rhetoric*. London, 1767. Print.

Graves, Frank Pierrepont. *A Student's History of Education*. New York: Macmillan, 1916. Print.

Harvey, Gabriel. *Ciceronianus*. Trans. Clarence A. Forbes. Ed. Harold S. Wilson. Lincoln: U of Nebraska P, 1945. (Original work published 1577.) Print.

Harvey, Gabriel. *Rhetor*. London, 1577. Print.

Hawes, Stephen. *Pastime of Pleasure*. Ed. William Edward Mead. London: Early English Text Society, 1928. (Original work published 1509.) Print.

Hill, Adam Sherman. *The Principles of Rhetoric and Their Application*. New York: Harper, 1878. Print.

Holmes, John. *The Art of Rhetoric Made Easy: In Two Books*. London, 1739. Print.

Horner, Winifred Bryan. "The Eighteenth Century." *The Present State of Scholarship in Historical and Contemporary Rhetoric*. Ed. Winifred Bryan Horner. Columbia: U of Missouri P, 1983. 101–133. Print.

Howell, Wilbur Samuel. *Logic and Rhetoric in England, 1500–1700*. New York: Russell and Russell, 1961. Print.

Howes, Raymond. Review of *College Handbook of Composition* by Edwin Woolley and F. Scott. *English Journal* 17.10 (1928): 864–865. Print.

Hudson, Hoyt H. "Jewel's Oration against Rhetoric." *The Quarterly Journal of Speech* 14 (1928): 374–392. Print.

Jamieson, Alexander. *A Grammar of Rhetoric and Polite Literature*. London; G. and W. B. Whittaker, 1818. Print.

Johnson, Nan. *Nineteenth-century Rhetoric in North America*. Carbondale: Southern Illinois UP, 1991. Print.

Kennedy, George A. *Classical Rhetoric and Its Christian and Secular Tradition from Ancient to Modern Times*. Chapel Hill: The U of North Carolina P, 1980. Print.

Kuhn, Thomas. *The Structure of Scientific Revolutions*. 2nd ed. Chicago, IL: U of Chicago P, 1970. Print.

Libanius' *Progymnasmata*. Web. 23 Jun 2007.

Ludham, John. *The Practise of preaching, Otherwise Called The Pathway to the Pulpet: Conteyning an excellent Method how to frame Divine Sermons*. London, 1577. Print.

Manly, John Matthew, and Edith Rickert. "The Writing of English." Ed. John Brereton. *The Origins of Composition Studies in the American College, 1875–1925*. Pittsburgh, PA: U of Pittsburgh P, 1995. 429–436. Print.

Marrou, Henri Irenee. *A History of Education in Antiquity*. Trans. George Lamb. Madison: U of Wisconsin P, 1982. Print.

Mason, John. *An Essay on Elocution or Pronunciation*. London: Cooper and Wilson, 1748. Print.

McCrimmon, James. *Writing with a Purpose*. Boston, MA: Heath, 1949. Print.

McComiskey, Bruce. "Dissoi Logoi (Dialexeis)." *Encyclopedia of Rhetoric and Composition: Communication from Ancient Times to the Information Age*. Ed. Theresa Enos. New York and London: Garland, 1996. 197–98. Print.

Morgan, Aron. "Medieval Rhetoric." *Encyclopedia of Rhetoric and Composition: Communication from Ancient Times to the Information Age*. Ed. Theresa Enos. New York and London: Garland, 1996. 429–35. Print.

Murphy, James J. *Rhetoric in the Middle Ages: A History of Rhetorical Theory from St. Augustine to the Renaissance*. Berkeley and Los Angeles: U of California P, 1974. Print.

Quintilian. *Institutio Oratoria*. Trans. H. E. Butler. 4 vols. Cambridge, MA: Harvard UP, 1968. (Original work published 95 CE.) Print.

Peacham, Henry. *The Garden of Eloquence Conteyning the Figures of Grammer and Rhetorick*. London: H. Jackson, 1577. Print.

Priestley, Joseph. *A Course on Oratory and Criticism*. Ed. David Potter. Carbondale: Southern Illinois UP, 1965. (Original work published 1777.) Print.

Rainolde, Richard. *The Foundacion of Rhetorike*. Ed. R. C. Alston. Menston, England: ScholarPress, 1972. (Original work published 1563.) Print.

Ramus, Peter. *Arguments in Rhetoric Against Quintilian*. Trans. Carole Newlands. Ed. James J. Murphy. De Kalb: Northern Illinois UP, 1983. (Original work published 1549.) Print.

—. *Brutinae Quaestiones*. Trans. Carole Newlands. Ed. James J. Murphy. Davis, CA: Hermagoras Press, 1992. (Original work published 1547.) Print.

—. *Dialectique*. Paris: Andre Wechel, 1555. Print.

Robinson, Thomas M. *Contrasting Arguments: An Edition of the Dissoi Logi*. New York: Arno Press, 1979. Print

Roen, Duane, Maureen Goggin, and Jennifer Clary-Lemon. "Development of Writing Teachers through the Ages." *Handbook of Writing Research*. Ed. Charles Bazerman. New York: Lawrence Erlbaum, 2008. 347–364. Print.

Scott, Fred Newton, and Joseph V. Denny. *Paragraph-Writing*. Ann Arbor, MI: Register Publishing Company, The Inland Press, 1891. Print.

Sheridan, Thomas. *Course of Lectures on Elocution Together with Two Dissertations on Language*. New York: Benjamin Blom, 1968. (Original work published 1762.) Print.

Sherry, Richard. *Treatise of the Figures of Grammar and Rhetoric*. London, 1555. Print.

Sherry, Richard. *A Treatise of Schemes and Tropes*. Ed. H. W. Hildebrandt. Gainesville: U of Florida P, 1961. (Original work published 1550.) Print.

Smith, Adam. *Lectures on Rhetoric and Belles Lettres Delivered in the University of Glasgow by Adam Smith Reported by a Student in 1762–63*. Ed. David Potter. Carbondale: Southern Illinois UP, 1971. Print.

Steeves, Harrison Ross, and Frank Humphrey Ristine. *Representative Essays in Modern Thought: A Basis for Composition*. Ed. John Brereton. *The Origins of Composition Studies in the American College, 1875–1925*. Pittsburgh, PA: U of Pittsburgh P, 1995. 386–389. Print.

Strunk, William. "The Elements of Style." Ed. John Brereton. *The Origins of Composition Studies in the American College, 1875–1925*. Pittsburgh, PA: U of Pittsburgh P, 1995. 406–415. Print.

Swarthy, Stanley. Review of *Composition for College Students* by Joseph M. Thomas; Frederick A. Manchester; Franklin W. Scott. *English Journal* 12.3 (1923): 218–19. Print.

Tacitus. *Dialogus de Oratoribus*. Cambridge: Cambridge UP, 2001. (Original work published *ca.* 102 CE.) Print.

Thomas, Joseph, Frederick Manchester, and Franklin Scott. *Composition for College Students*. New York: MacMillian, 1924. Print.

Tibbetts, A. M. "'Argument' in Nineteenth Century American Rhetoric Textbooks" *College Composition and Communication* 18.5 (1967): 236–241. Print.

Traversagni, Lorenze Ruglielmo. *Nova Rhetorica*. London: William Caxton, 1480. Print.

Vygotsky, Lev. *Thought and Language*. Cambridge, MA: The M.I.T. Press, 1962. Print.

Walker, John. *Elements of Elocution. Being the Substance of a Course of Lectures on the Art of Reading: Delivered at several Colleges in the University of Oxford*. London, 1781. Print.

Ward, John. *A System of Oratory, Delivered in a Course of Lectures Publicly Read at Gresham College*. London, 1759. Print.

Welch, Kathleen E. "Writing Instruction in Ancient Athens After 450 B.C." *A Short History of Writing Instruction: From Ancient Greece to Twentieth-Century America*. Ed. James J. Murphy. Davis, CA: Hermagoras Press, 1990. 1–18. Print.

Wendell, Barrett. *English Composition: Eight Lectures Given at the Lowell Institute*. New York: Scribner's, 1891. Print.

Whately, Richard. *Elements of Rhetoric*. London, 1828. Print.

Wilson, Thomas. *The Arte of Rhetorique*. Ed. G. H. Mair. Oxford: Clarendon Press, 1909. (Original work published 1553.) Print.

Witherspoon, John. *Lectures on Moral Philosophy and Eloquence*. Philadelphia, 1810. Print.

Woods, Marjorie Curry. "The Teaching of Writing in Medieval Europe." *A Short History of Writing Instruction: From Ancient Greece to Twentieth-Century America*. Ed. James J. Murphy. Davis, CA: Hermagoras Press, 1990. 77–94. Print.

Woolley, Edwin. "Excerpts of *Handbook of Composition*." Ed. John Brereton. *The Origins of Composition Studies in the American College, 1875–1925*. Pittsburgh, PA: U of Pittsburgh P, 1995. 359–372. Print.

Woolley, Edwin, Franklin Scott, and Frederick Bracher. *College Handbook of Composition*. Boston, MA: Heath, 1937. Print.

8 Disciplining Technology: A Selective Annotated Bibliography

Marcia Kmetz, Robert Lively,
Crystal Broch-Colombini, and Thomas Black

It is difficult to talk about technology in the classroom in the twenty-first century without having the discussion turn to computers and online pedagogical practices. However, as seen in the previous chapters and in our classrooms, we are surrounded by other forms of technology that have had, and continue to have, a profound impact on the teaching profession. We observe how the dusty blackboard made way for the cleaner and more legible dry-erase board; how the projector, which warbled through film strips, faded from view as the VCR and cassette emerged; how projectors and VCRs then gave way to the DVD, which, even as this is being written, is losing ground to internet file sharing sites like YouTube. Desks, which used to be little more than inexpensive chairs with a table bolted to them, are now ergonomically designed to promote posture and comfort and lessen distraction. Lecture halls are designed to be acoustically responsive so that even soft speakers can be clearly heard in every corner. The most modern of classrooms are wirelessly mechanized with technology such as visual presentation systems allowing instruction at the push of a button. In short, when we look closely at our classrooms, we see that technological advancements are both omnipresent and critical in assisting us with engaging our students. At least we hope.

The preceding chapters show that technology in the field of Rhetoric and Composition is not just a modern phenomenon. For better or worse technology has had a significant impact on our instruction and research, though this impact has at times been behind the scenes and affected us without our awareness. This chapter looks at the less visible aspects of the Rhetoric/Composition knowledge base and examines how our field has historically and currently theorized non-computer technologies and how those technologies affect our evolving pedagogies. It provides an overview of the major journals in Rhetoric and Composition and offers a selected bibliography of those articles that cover technologies before and beside the computer or related applications. We sought technology in the form of concrete devices rather than discussions involving abstract concepts. While this is a not a comprehensive review, we find the articles represented in this collection provide a substantial contribution regarding noncomputer technology, as well as a continuum of how technology plays a critical role in the development of composition and rhetoric as a discipline.

While the purpose of this chapter is not to provide analysis of these articles, we have come to some initial conclusions. First, and probably foremost, the discussion is not uniform across the discipline. In certain journals the discussion of technology is almost nonexistent, while in others, generally those considered more pedagogy-based, the discussion of technology is continuous and thorough. Second, we noted that frequently teachers and scholars explained the use of a particular technology in the classroom without examining the impacts of that technology on their individual theories or on the field's collective praxis.

College Composition and Communication

College Composition and Communication, an early pioneer in journals for the field of Rhetoric and Composition, has demonstrated a clear commitment to the study of how new theories and technologies affect the teaching of college-level English. First published in March 1950, the journal originally centered around the conference on college composition and communication, specifically devoting one full issue per year to the happenings at that conference. As the field grew larger, however, the journal became a space for contestations about new practices in the classroom, new theories about learning and writing instruction, and new ideas about technological devices. In general, articles on technology discussed methods that had been used over a number of quarters or semesters with some success. On a theoretical level, the emerging technologies were clearly tied to larger movements in the field. A primary concern addressed in many articles was how to make use of limited faculty and limited resources without sacrificing quality of education in the face of rising enrollment rates. The numbers of new students entering universities created a challenge for the field as a whole and the technology recommended to deal with the issue was television, either in early forms of distance education through public access or closed-circuit television or through lectures done by a full faculty member and broadcast to the multiple sections of freshman composition at least once per week in an effort to overcome the lack of PhDs in the classroom and to unify the freshman composition experience. As one might expect, some technologies were more useful than others. While a multiple-response device is discussed once and audiotapes enter the discussion twice, these are quickly discarded as ineffective or inefficient. Television and film take more space here, though, as the many ways these technologies might be used are explored and as the technologies enter discussions of literacy, particularly the new concept of visual literacy.

Mathews, Mitford M. "The Freshman and His Dictionary." *College Composition and Communication* 6.4 (1955): 187–190.

Arguing that dictionaries are far more "complicated and capable" than freshmen understand, Mitford M. Mathews calls for a classroom program emphasizing the uses of a dictionary. Such a program would include a background understanding of the "big four" dictionaries—*Oxford English Dictionary*, *English Dialect Dictionary*, the twelve-volume *Century Dictionary*, and *Webster*—as well as beginning information about the history of the English language and the standard usages of a dictionary including guidance on spelling, meaning, and pronunciation. This program is meant to encourage students to become curious about words and their meanings and histories.

Hoagland, John H. "Closed-Circuit TV at New York University." *College Composition and Communication* 7.2 (1956): 67–70.

John H. Hoagland describes a 1956 CCCCs panel on the new technology of teaching through closed-circuit television. The panel was conducted by educators at New York University who compared the invention of television to the earlier invention of movable type, adding that many had feared the technology of printing would mean an "end for true culture," a common criticism of early television. They provided a sample lesson framed by a discussion about the uses of the new technology, ultimately concluding it might best be used for science courses with closed-circuit TV for composition courses requiring "more ingenuity."

Fidone, William G. "Teaching Pilot Courses Over Public Television Channels." *College Composition and Communication* 7.4 (1956): 204–205.

Because rising enrollment numbers were requiring alternative ways of delivering writing education, William G. Fidone reports on a writing course offered over public television: "Language for the Layman." This course was a predecessor to distance education offering on-air lectures and the opportunity to mail in assignments. It was aimed at those not typically able to participate in university education; Fidone cites housewives and farmers as examples. Problems arose, however, specifically the exclusion of live audiences, the necessity of an instructor who is also a skilled performer, and teaching "enmeshed with stage directions."

"Closed-Circuit Television in Teaching Communication Skills." *College Composition and Communication* 8.3 (1957): 187–189.

This article describes recent experiments in composition instruction using closed-circuit television, specifically experiments at New York University, Penn State, and Evanston Township High School. While the authors note that the effect on students had not yet been determined, they argue that closed-circuit television may be preferable to large lecture courses. The authors cite benefits suggested by members of a workshop panel on the subject, namely that television could be beneficial for speech training, yet they also describe anticipated problems such as the limitations for reading and thinking skills and the impediment of discussion. They further note that this technology may increase a need for "prime talent for TV instruction," something they find more rare than teaching talent in general.

Wykoff, George S. "Current Solutions for Teaching Maximum Numbers with Limited Faculty." *College Composition and Communication* 9.2 (1958): 76–80.

Given predictions of ever-increasing enrollment rates for colleges and limited numbers of faculty, George S. Wykoff outlines some classroom aids that may increase efficiency in the classroom and effective use of faculty. Aids mentioned that are technological in nature include television (here focusing on both closed-circuit and commercial) and film or slides.

Paulits, F. Joseph. "Slides and Composition." *College Composition and Communication* 10.1 (1959): 47–50.

Joseph F. Paulits outlines a use of color slides in the composition classroom. By using images he took on a trip to Europe, he engaged students in discussions about creating a visual image for readers, distinguishing what they see in fine detail, and scene-setting. He then incorporated a fairly simple image and asked students to write about it, assuming they would oversimplify it given the difficulty of the earlier images used for analysis. The students read their compositions describing the scene the following class period while classmates compared the text to the actual image. He continues this process throughout the semester to instruct on a variety of writerly purposes.

Remington, Fred. "Television: The Over-Criticized Medium." *College Composition and Communication* 10.2 (1959): 95–98.

In a CCCC luncheon address, Fred Remington, a five-year veteran of the television industry, argues that while television programmers are perhaps not doing the best job possible in promoting quality entertainment, they are still not responsible for the mass ills of society. He cites the connection between the criticisms launched at the television industry and those piled on educators, noting that neither is ultimately responsible for the condition of society. Instead, he argues that for the discerning person there is an abundance of quality programming and that viewers should approach the selection of television programs with the same careful critique as they approach books.

Bellamy, John E. "Teaching Composition by Television." *College Composition and Communication* 11.1 (1960): 36–39.

While noting that lessons broadcast over television have certain limitations, specifically that the distance between the instructor and his or her students is enhanced and that it in some cases eliminates effective discussions, John E. Bellamy still argues for the ultimate effectiveness of well-designed television lectures based on a two quarter experiment for Oregon State System of Higher Education. If the courses are designed around ideas rather than craft lectures and if the lessons are adequately explained and standards are articulated and enforced, then television lectures can be an effective way to reduce the work of instructors in the classroom.

Houghton, Donald E. "Paperback Research: Some Shortcomings." *College Composition and Communication* 11.4 (1960): 203–206.

Donald E. Houghton challenges the usefulness of the newly designed paperback anthologies for beginning composition courses. He argues that unless the course is designed to teach students how to read and respond to literature, the anthologies have a number of setbacks including an increased ability for students to plagiarize, a decreased ability for students to engage in authentic research processes on a topic of interest to them, and an inability for students to see the "messiness" of research from false starts to necessary narrowing of topics. He ultimately determines that paperback anthologies place students in a "strait jacket of controlled sources."

Lambert, Robert. "Filmgraphics: Documentaries on Campus." *College Composition and Communication* 14.1 (1963): 25–27.

Robert Lambert describes his university's efforts to promote a relatively unexplored genre of film: the documentary. His campus held free weekly viewings of differing types of documentaries in an effort to promote the genre as well as get students engaged in discussion. In a time of much talk about the value or damage of film in the classroom, Lambert stresses that this genre offers a focus on craftsmanship that might be useful for composition instruction.

Dye, Robert. "The Film: Sacred and Profane." *College Composition and Communication* 15.1 (1964): 41–43.

In a scathing critique of the direction of film, Robert Dye suggests that the majority of contemporary films were "prostituted literature" rather than sacred in scope or content. Yet this profane nature offers students and teachers the opportunity to consider their own response to the sacred and to intellectualize the profane. These films can, therefore, be introduced in classrooms in order to consider literary art or societal criticism, to comparatively study the form, and/or to discuss film as a "form of statement."

Baker, William D. "Film as Sharpener of Perception." *College Composition and Communication* 15.1 (1964): 44–45.

Arguing that film analysis is a new method of rhetorical criticism, William D. Baker discusses his use of short films in the classroom to teach student writers how to be "deliberate artists" like poets and film producers. Baker begins his course with a study of the language of film critique followed by analysis of short films for technique and discussions involving the subjects of detail, generalization, theme generation, and comparative analysis. He then shows students how their understanding of these skills in film can be translated into effective composition and critique of writing.

Kallsen, T.J. "Hi-Fi Theme Grading." *College Composition and Communication* 16.2 (1965): 124–126.

While instructors at Stephen F. Austin State College continued to mark on student papers with regard to grammar errors, they recorded their longer comments concerning logic, evidence, organization, or style onto phonograph records for the students to listen to while they revised their papers. Drawbacks were noted, particularly that records cannot replace personal conferences and that a method for efficiency needs to be developed by each individual instructor, yet the author contends that content and organization improved more than with typical paper comments. Still, T.J. Kallsen concludes that this method is likely more useful for advanced composition courses than for freshman composition.

Forsyth, Joseph. "Composition, the Overhead, and the Team." *College Composition and Communication* 16.3 (1965): 174–176.

Joseph Forsyth outlines the implications of a new course, *Contemporary Composition* for the overhead projector, as it was applied to five composition courses at New Mexico State University. These sections were taught by three regular instructors, the department head, and a graduate assistant and were designed so each instructor met with his or her class twice weekly and all students from the five sections met together once weekly for instructional lessons taught on the overhead. Anonymous end-of-semester surveys suggested some benefit to this model of teaching in terms of student learning and classroom efficiency, though Forsyth notes that many components affect student performance.

Pirtle, Wayne G. "The Use of a Multiple Response Device in the Teaching of Remedial English." *College Composition and Communication* 16.3 (1965): 176–177.

Merced College developed a multiple integrated response device for use in writing classrooms in order to increase students' participation. The device, with switches at each desk connected to a control panel at the instructor's desk, allows instructors to ask impromptu multiple choice questions that provide immediate feedback concerning student understanding of the current lesson and provide instant reinforcement to students. The entire class can see the correct answers on the switchboard, increasing competition and motivation to achieve according to Wayne G. Pirtle.

Nall, Kline A. "Beefing Up the T.A. Program with ETV." *College Composition and Communication* 17.5 (1966): 255–258.

Kline A. Nall, chairman of Freshman English at Texas Tech University, cites rising student enrollments and increasing reliance on TAs (1000% increase over ten years) as the causes for their work to unify instructional methods in their freshman courses. To accomplish this, they broadcast common lessons over the university's public television station for one hour per week. The lessons, designed by Nall, were intended to provide a full professor to each of the nearly four hundred classrooms at least one hour a week and to provide additional mentoring to the TAs as they watched a senior professor provide instruction to their classes. In this way, Nall argues that television can move from the periphery of the classroom into a more vital role.

Greene, Anne, and James Quivey. "The Use of a Grid in the Construction of a Multiple-Choice Examination for the Composition Program." *College Composition and Communication* 18.2 (1967): 67–71.

Northern Illinois University, in an effort to make better use of their "mass objective final examination" in all Freshman Composition courses, created a grid (a two-way chart that relates course content to course objectives) to insure coverage of the course material as well as a balance between the compositional aspects tested. While changes were made to the device throughout the process of construction, the authors found that the grid made them consider the process more intellectually and that it ultimately measured the aspects it was designed to measure.

"Brooklyn College 'Audiovisual Literacy' Project." *College Composition and Communication* 20.2 (1969): 158.

This article describes a three-year study examining the effects of audio-visual instruction on the reading motivation and skills of students from disadvantaged areas. Taking as his premise that these students assimilate information first through television and the media, Dr. Levison (the researcher) delineates a reading instruction program using films that are "works of art" first, followed by student production of film or tape recordings, "feedback" in the form of transcriptions of the students' words from the recordings, and, ultimately, reading instruction from teachers trained in audio-visual literacy. This was written at the beginning of the project, so no results or implications are suggested.

Briand, Paul. "Turned On: Multi-Media and Advanced Composition." *College Composition and Communication* 21.3 (1970): 267–269.

After disappointing results in his attempt to teach the craft of writing, Paul Briand turned to multimedia. He initially considered correcting themes on film for the student to watch, yet was discouraged because of the cost and time commitment. He did, however, begin to grade papers on audiotape so students could have a record of both his comments and their progression as writers. He used television recordings to note examples of errors in student papers so he could use those televised corrections in future courses. He also made use of a three-screen projection with 35 mm slide transparencies for lecture material as well as presentations to attend to students' visual literacy. He ultimately decides these technologies are useful only insofar as they help teach the skill of writing.

Murphy, Sharon. "TV Footage in the Composition Classroom." *College Composition and Communication* 23.1 (1972): 50–53.

Sharon Murphy offers an argument for using public service announcements and television commercials to study written and oral persuasion in composition noting that when materials are selected for their relevance (of content and form) to college level students, interest in the topic peaks. How the materials are crafted, particularly public service ads, also provides valuable lessons to students. Ultimately, this approach is meant to build "a critical familiarity with these electronic messages" that might allow students and teachers to improve in the technical aspects of writing as well as the work of critiquing everyday messages.

Sawyer, Thomas M. "Rhetoric in an Age of Science and Technology." *College Composition and Communication* 23.5 (1972):390–398.

In an age of science and technology, says Thomas M. Sawyer, educators are faced not only with an information explosion but also with diverse student bodies (in terms of professional interests) that cannot all be attended to in a freshman course on literature or grammar. Yet in order for the public to keep track of scientific innovations and to critique the direction science is taking our society, scientists should be able to speak to a larger public in clear language. Typically, science writing is inherently functional, meant to be acted on, and contains three rhetorical characteristics: a deductive system, an assumption that a reader will understand the underlying premises that inform the work, and a sequence of symbols that make sense of the propositions and deductions. These generally serve fellow scientists, however, rather than being comprehensible to the lay public. Thus Sawyer argues that courses should address writing skills that match the needs of scientists while producing work that is understandable for those in differing fields of study.

Bernett, Esther, and Sandra Thomason. "The Cassette Slide Show in Required Composition." *College Composition and Communication* 25.5 (1974): 426–430.

Esther Bernett and Sandra Thomason describe an alternative assignment they offer in composition courses: an audio-visual presentation. While the majority of students choose a standard term paper, a handful of students elect to prepare this presentation using a scripted and recorded narrative, photos advanced through a slide projector, and sound effects. The authors found that students who lacked motivation to write standard papers often responded well to this assignment and that the presentation taught writing and research skills along with skills in organization and public speaking.

Primeau, Ronald. "Film Editing and the Revision Process: Student as Self-Editor." *College Composition and Communication* 25.5 (1974): 405–410.

Ronald Primeau argues that students have been adversely affected by the debate over whether writing is a craft or an act of genius, but suggests that a more concerted effort in the teaching of revision might convince our students that writing can be taught and learned. His strategy is to use the process of film editing to demonstrate to students how to see their drafts differently, noting that the angle of the camera, the timing of shots, and the sound patterns can be used to demonstrate revision. He particularly advises Dziga Vertov's "kino-eye" technique, a technique that assumes the camera is a tool for creative note-taking on film and then, following the observational stage, the filmmaker establishes the "order of exposition." This can support a "patchwork" philosophy of revision that helps students see writing as an ongoing process, as the combining of parts to make meaningful wholes.

Adams, Dale, and Robert Kline. "The Use of Films in Teaching Composition." *College Composition and Communication* 26.3 (1975): 258–262.

Dale Adams and Robert Kline suggest that long-standing barriers to the use of film in the classroom—including length, scarcity, cost, and administrative red tape—were no longer as prevalent and that the values of the films to the classroom should be considered. Those values are the immediacy of impact, understanding unrelated to reading comprehension, increased student confidence and originality, the "natural appeal" of film to younger students, the variety of writing approaches that can make use of film, increased scholarship on and critique of film, and the inherent value of the visual image. While they are clear that the use of film will not automatically or even eventually repair all the challenges of the composition course, they do suggest that film can enhance students' experiences.

Barnes, Verle. "Eight Basic Considerations for the Teaching of Film."
  College Composition and Communication 27.1 (1976): 32–35.

While Verle Barnes is primarily addressing the teaching of an entire
course in film, he believes the eight considerations are relevant for
composition courses as well. He cites those considerations as preparation (first of instructor then of students), an attitude of independence
toward the discipline, the quality of the film, the enjoyment or entertainment value, the amount of time necessary to show part or all of
the film, a balanced schedule with allowed time for other assignments
and activities, and the course budget. With these considerations met,
Barnes finds that the value of film far outweighs the challenges.

Struck, H.R. "Twenty Well-Tested Films for Freshman Writing Courses." *College Composition and Communication* 27.1 (1976): 47–50.

Basing his assessment on the criteria of usefulness, H.R. Struck outlines twenty films that have been successful in required composition
classes at Michigan State University. While he includes arguments and
uses for each of the twenty and a potential schedule for these films,
much of this piece centers on arguments for use of film in the classroom, particularly uses that sequence into assignments. An example is
a "serious" film that leads into three assignments: a detailed recollec-
tion of a scene from the film, a critique of the film that shows how it
aligns with other ideas or characters, and an autobiographical paper.
The final paper offers students an opportunity to use the sensory and
analytical skills learned from the film and the first two assignments to
explore their own personal stories.

Meyer, Russell J., and Barton W. Galle, Jr. "How to Build a Composition Slide File." *College Composition and Communication* 27.3
  (1976): 285–287.

Russell J. Meyer and Barton W. Galle, Jr. showcase their institution's
"composition slide file," a collection of slides containing authentic student examples of common writing problems, arguing that the use of
them allows the instructor to keep students focused on the lecture.
They describe in detail the methods of developing bound copy-sheets
as guides to the collection as well as preparing the slides. Because these
slides were shared by the entire writing program and were susceptible

to wear, the authors note they are meant to be used only as an occasional class activity.

Popovich, Helen Hauser. "From Tape to Type: An Approach to Composition." *College Composition and Communication* 27.3 (1976): 283–285.

In Helen Hauser Popovich's writing course, she made use of a cassette recorder to tape students reading their texts so they would pay more particular attention to organization, punctuation, sentence patterning, repetition, and "stiltedness" in style and dialogue. She reports that because some recordings were chosen for classroom discussion and because students were required to read their work, they discovered the connection between the theoretical aspects of writing and practical applications and they worked more diligently at writing.

COLLEGE ENGLISH

College English has a long and storied history as one of the most influential journals in postsecondary education. Most of the early articles in *College English* deal primarily with literature. Even the few early articles concerning technology argue for their uses in teaching literature-based courses. However, outside of recent articles on computers, technology is never really explored in *College English*. Even though we are sure it invariably was used in the college classroom, the conversation of that usage is severely lacking from *CE*'s pages.

Weingarten, Samuel. "The Use of Phonograph Recordings in Teaching Shakespeare." *College English* 1.1 (1939): 45–61.

Samuel Weingarten argues in this article that the use of phonograph recordings will better help the students understand the theatrical aspects of Shakespeare's plays. Since literature classes often neglect the performance aspects of the plays, he argues that recordings can open a new dimension in teaching Shakespeare.

Christensen, Glenn J. "A Decade of Radio Drama." *College English* 8.4 (1947): 179–185.

In this essay, Glenn J. Christensen examines the decade of drama on the radio. Specifically, he looks at Archibald MacLeish's "stage of words theory" to illustrate the performance and transforming power of radio drama in relation to the power of the spoken word without indulgence in sound effects of props of any kind.

Hazard, Patrick D. "Technological Change and the Humanities Curriculum." *College English*
16.7 (1955): 435–443.
Patrick D. Hazard's bold essay challenges teachers in the humanities to throw away their prejudices against technology in the classroom and view technology as a potentially liberating experience. After all, he contends, technology has allowed the creation of inexpensive paperbacks, radios, and phonograph records for use in the classroom. He argues that technology can engage students in new and exciting ways.

Feinstein, George W. "The Strange Invention at Yahoo Polytechnic." *College English* 17.6 (1956): 355–357.

George W. Feinstein's comic article discusses the advancement of an imaginary IBM scoring machine. This marvel of technology can correct student themes and give great, and pertinent, advice to the students in a fraction of the time the professors can. The teachers enjoy this new stress free teaching life; that is, until the scoring machine is fed the papers written by the "star athletes" and is irreparably damaged.

Knepler, Henry W. "English via Television." *College English* 18.1 (1956): 1–11.

Henry W. Knepler's article is visionary in its scope in light of our distance education programs today. He explores the idea of using the new technology of television as a delivery device for English studies. He examines the use of closed-circuit television as a means of broadcasting lectures and kinescopic films to produce an effective English curriculum over great distances. The cost, as he states, is quite prohibitive, however. He estimates that to set up his visionary distance education, it would cost more than $250,000. Quite a sum for the 1950s.

Ward, F. Earl. "Teaching Poetry with Tape Recordings." *College English* 20.1 (1958): 21–23.

In this essay, Professor Ward contends that to truly appreciate poetry, it must be heard. Therefore, he argues that poetry must make use of tape recordings in the English classroom. He urges poetry teachers to make their own recordings of poems to let the students hear the lilting quality of the rhythms.

Ong, Walter J. "Media Transformations: The Talked Book." *College English* 34.3 (1972): 405–410.

Walter J. Ong meditates on the use of new technology and what it means to author something. In his article, he narrates producing a book without his writing anything. He was interviewed, taped, called, taped, and finally asked to review the completed interview transcribed and edited by someone else to be printed. He wonders at how this will eventually change the medium of textual production

Klammer, Enno. "Cassettes in the Classroom." *College English* 35.2 (1973): 179–180+.

Enno Klammer uses the idea of oral response to help grade student papers. While reading through essays, he speaks his comments onto a cassette and hands the essay and the cassette to the student for personalized and fairly quick turnaround on his grading. Klammer argues that the students will feel more compelled to revise if they hear the teacher's comments instead of just seeing the comments on the page.

Hunt, Russel A. "Technological Gift-Horse: Some Reflections on the Teeth of Cassette-Marking." *College English* 36.5 (1975): 581–585.

This practical essay argues that cassette responses to student writing may not be all that sensational after all. Russel A. Hunt explains of his use of cassettes in his writing courses, and how liberating he should have felt—except he ended up lugging around a heavy cassette recorder and a myriad of tapes. He found he was not able to quickly go back and review student writing without having to listen to a pile of tapes to find what he was looking for. However, once he vents these shortcomings, he presents a nice argument for the use of recorders based on a comparison of time spent marking papers, both orally and written. He concludes by saying written comments are clearly on the way out.

Andrews, Barbara, and David Hakken. "Educational Technology: A Theoretical Discussion." *College English* 39.1 (1977): 68–108.

This Marxist-leaning article discusses the theoretical framework of technology instruction in schools. Barbara Andrews and David Hakken argue that education has become an industry, and as such, the typical shortcomings of business will be manifested in public education. While the authors see technology as potentially liberating, they also note it can be isolating and impersonal.

COMPOSITION STUDIES (FRESHMAN ENGLISH NEWS)

As the oldest independent periodical in its field, *Composition Studies* (formerly *Freshman English News*) began in 1972 as a forum to report on and discuss the happenings in Freshman English across the country. Its modern aim is to explore the complexities of teaching, theorizing, and administering college-level composition courses. The early pages, then, focused more on practice and that is apparent in our review of the few technology pieces available in early issues. Largely, these articles focus on uses of technology in the classroom or critiques of earlier articles (appearing in other journals) about those same technologies. Thus, this journal serves as primary space for discussion and debate on newer technologies. Because the journal began in the early 1970s, there are few pieces about technologies prior to the computer, yet those articles are telling of the larger discussions happening in the field.

Comprone, Joseph. "Using Film within the Composing Process." *Freshman English News* 10.1 (1981): 21–24.

Referencing contemporary work done on the composing process of writers, particularly that of Janet Emig and Peter Elbow, Joseph Comprone argues that because composing has been demonstrated as a recursive cyclical activity, an effective use of film in the classroom can be a problem solving approach. Such an approach allows instructors to gather hypotheses from students based on their perceptions of the film, help students break down those hypotheses into "operators" used to reexamine the film, and use analogy to help students make connections between the film and their lives. These connections are used to move students into the "middle stage" of composing. Comprone suggests that film supports this process by demonstrating to students that language (visual or textual) is "manipulated and controlled by a composer."

Rocha, Mark. "The Unsurprising Case against Television Literacy." *Freshman English News* 17.1 (1988): 27–29.

Mark Rocha centers his "unsurprising" argument against an earlier study about the benefits of television in writing classrooms. Arguing that the article supposes an antagonism toward television that is no longer prevalent (but for E. D. Hirsch, Jr.), ignores contextual limitations for high school teachers (including the need to teach toward the "back to basics movement"), and seems unaware of research that disproves the alleged tie between television and literacy, Rocha suggests that television has created an audience with no rhetor. Thus the "urgent need" is to recreate rhetoricians rather than promote more work on audience participation. To do this we can study the interrelationship of text and performance.

COMPUTERS AND COMPOSITION

Computers and Composition covers computer-related theory and practice in relation to the Composition field. The articles included in this chapter represent how the boom of computer technology has created an interest in looking into historical applications of technologies prior to the computer. With the multitude of technology applications available for instructors today and the resulting confusion, and sometimes resistance, *Computers and Composition* provides articles that examine how technology has previously been received (with familiar resistance) and incorporated into the composition field.

Hass, Christina. "On the Relationship Between Old and New Technologies." *Computers and Composition* 16.2 (1999): 209–28.

Christina Hass provides a review of technologies as they operated within the workplace before and up to modern technology (computers). Using case studies that analyze certain technologies such as the telephone, facsimiles, and other printed texts, Hass seeks to demonstrate how Vygotsky's models, such as the replacement model and the straightforward model, are not adequate to illustrate the relationship between old and new technologies. The models proposed by Vygotsky suggest old technologies are simply replaced by new technologies and power structures of these technologies remain relatively stable in the workplace. Using Bijker's theory of socio-technical change, Hass asserts a more complex analysis of technology and the related social structures. This article calls on the composition community to look at modern technology not as a replacement for old technology, but as artifacts of social change.

Smith, Catherine F. "Thomas Jefferson's Computer." *Computers and Composition* 13.1 (1996): 5–21.

Engaging the metaphor of writing in a new century, as modern teachers seem to be engaging in the twenty-first century by teaching in digital environments, Catherine F. Smith shows that Thomas Jefferson was in somewhat the same situation when engaged with starting a new nation. Using Jefferson's vast writing examples as a framework provides a look at how he composed his writing life and how this applies to the modern day computer. Looking at these examples, Jefferson is seen using technologies to promote democracy and provide more freedoms for Americans. This is in contrast to more postmodern Foucauldian pessimistic views that technology is a form of relinquished control.

Kalmbach, James. "From Liquid Paper to Typewriters: Some Historical Perspectives on Technology in the Classroom." *Computers and Composition* 13.1 (1996): 57–68.

Technologies have always had their place in the in the composition classroom, but rarely are these technologies acknowledged. It wasn't until computers came along when teachers began to take notice of the impact technology has on their pedagogical practices, especially considering the speed and complexity with which technology progresses. However, looking at how instructors incorporated technology into their classrooms before computers provides some insight into how they work modern technology into pedagogical structures. Using examples such as the printing press, typewriters, and liquid paper as early technological examples, we see that many of the arguments concerning technology in the classroom are nothing new or unique to the twenty-first century. Yet the ultimate argument is not how technology affects our pedagogical practices, but how technology fits with our educational philosophy and whether it helps us or hinders us.

The English Journal

Almost one hundred years old, *The English Journal* has been at the forefront of the uses of technology in the classroom. This pedagogically-driven journal has captured the debates over uses of technology that have influenced us in the classroom and the profession. *The English Journal* has not only traced the developments of important media, such as film, radio, and television but the other experimental technologies that have faded into the murky past, such as the stereopticon, the delineascope, and the tachistoscope. At the nexus of classroom and technology, however, we must remember all of the teachers who have honestly tried to incorporate technology into their classrooms for the benefit of their students. While *The English Journal* is geared toward secondary education, the vibrancy of the debates and the creative uses of technology remind us of how much we owe to our predecessors in education. We were fascinated by the trends of articles as they appeared in the journal. First the technology was introduced, followed by a series of articles challenging its place and use in the classroom, and finally acceptance into the mainstream educational culture if it was successful, or the abrupt stop of articles if it wasn't.

Eaton, Mary Newell. "No Hero." *The English Journal* 1.1 (1912): 56–57.

This early article is about the use of the stereopticon in the classroom. (A stereopticon is a type of slide projector that could project an image in a slight 3-D effect). The article is very short, a mere three paragraphs, but it illustrates a very early use of technology in the literature classroom.

Monro, Kate M. "Blackboard Work and the Card System." *The English Journal* 7.7 (1918): 460–464.

Kate M. Monro argues that having students use the blackboard in the classroom is a way to engage "the elusive minds" of pupils. She insists the blackboard engages the students in ways that seatwork cannot. She demonstrates her ideas by using a punctuation and grammar exercise where students must correct a sentence she has given them on a small note card.

McCrosky, Cecile B. "The Administration of English in the High-School Curriculum." *English Journal* 7.2 (1918): 108–117.

While not exclusively dealing with technology in the classroom, this administrative report catalogues the resources, as well as the technology, found in a survey of Ohio schools by Mr. McCrosky.

Cunningham, Adelaide. "Teaching English with the Movies." *The English Journal* 12.7 (1923): 488–490.

This article was one of the first to offer a statistical report on students' grades for reading and watching a film. Adelaide Cunningham conducted an experiment of low performing students who had already failed a literature course. By watching the film in conjunction with the reading, student scores improved in tests and theme writing.

James, H. W. "The Effect of Handwriting upon Grading." *The English Journal* 16.3 (1927): 180–185.

While many in the modern day forget that penmanship requires technology, this fact is not lost on Dr. James. In this article, James explores the effects of sloppy handwriting on theme scores. He relates an experiment in which the same exams were sent out at two intervals, one neat the other sloppily written. Even though the content was the same, the neat ones received higher marks.

Abbott, Mary Allen. "Motion Picture Classics." *The English Journal* 21.8 (1932): 624–628.

This article discusses the idea of classic motion pictures, and their use for teachers in the English classroom. Mary Allen Abbott contends that identifying classic movies is possible because they should adhere to literary and theatrical standards.

Lewin, William. "Standards of Photoplay Appreciation." *The English Journal* 21.10 (1932): 799–810.

As the technology of movies, printing, and radios improved, William Lewin analyzes the argument that the advancement of photoplay technology can be used in the English classroom only if it adheres to good, clean standards. He encapsulates the debate of whether films should be viewed as morally correct or as works of art.

Lewin, William. "What Shall We Read about the Movies?" *The English Journal* 23.6 (1934): 497–500.

This brief annotated bibliography deals with viewing and evaluating films. Several titles explain how to objectively view and evaluate motion pictures.

Knight, Raymond. "Radio and the English Teacher." *The English Journal* 23.6 (1934): 504–506.

Raymond Knight's article discusses the use of radio in the classroom. He uses his radio program to correct the English of his "radio children." He sees this as a positive influence of the technology.

Dale, Edgar. "Teaching Motion Picture Appreciation." *The English Journal* 25.2 (1936): 113–120.

In this essay, Edgar Dale cites a statistic that over one thousand teachers used motion picture appreciation in the classroom. This shows the pervasiveness of films in the culture. Dale, however, argues that appreciation must go above just looking at the experience. He takes early steps in critical pedagogy by asking honest questions of racial portrayals and war propaganda in films.

Hibbit, George W. "Phonograph Recordings of Poets' Readings." *The English Journal* 25.6 (1936): 479–481.

In this short article, George W. Hibbit discusses the possible uses of phonograph recordings. Specifically, he argues for the recordings of successful American poets to preserve the spoken word for posterity. He points out his plans for recording Gertrude Stein and Robert Frost.

Phillips, Delight. "A Unit on the Use of Radio." *The English Journal* 26.1 (1937): 33–38.

Delight Phillips presents the rationale for a five-week unit on radio drama and production in the high school classroom. She gives the breakdown of the unit lesson in an outline form. She also gives examples of possible short stories to develop into radio drama.

Hurley, Richard James. "Movie and Radio—Friend and Foe." *The English Journal* 26.3 (1937): 205–211.

Richard James Hurley argues that movies are a friend to the students, while radio is detrimental to student success because it stops students from reading. He cites statistics that students view literary and historical movies in droves, so it is beneficial to education. Radio, on the other hand, dumbs down the young population. They listen to popular music, and they spend on average six hours a week listening to the radio.

Whitehead, Louise G. "The Motion Picture as a Medium of Class Instruction." *The English Journal* 26.4 (1937): 315–317.

This narrative essay explains the process Louise G. Whitehead went through trying to adapt literature in her class to make a film. She discusses the technical problems she encounters, as well as the problems of drafting scripts and scenes for a class mini-film.

Mersand, Joseph. "Radio Makes Readers." *The English Journal* 27.6 (1938): 469–475.

Joseph Mersand makes a counterargument circulating in educational literature and popular culture that radio destroys reading habits in youth. He argues, based on survey statistics, that radio drama of classic literature actually increases student reading of classic texts for pleasure.

Munz, Martin H. "Using the Projector in Written Composition." *The English Journal* 28.2 (1939): 130–131.

Martin H. Munz argues that the use of a delineascope, a device that can project a student paper onto a screen in the classroom (and looks like a small cannon), can help students with surface-level grammatical errors by correcting in class.

Gates, George G. "The Delineascope for Punctuation." *The English Journal* 28.7 (1939): 574–575.

George G. Gates contends that the use of the delineascope can be taken further than the article by Martin H. Munz suggests. He says the delineascope can be used in creative ways to teach problems in punctuation, and he supplies examples in the article.

Orndorff, Bernice. "English via the Air Waves." *The English Journal* 28.8 (1939): 619–628.

Bernice Orndorff challenges the previous literature and claims radio is a "natural" for the teaching of literature. She explores a list of seven goals radio use can achieve in the classroom, including thinking critically and expressing social responsibility.

Ginsberg, Walter. "Radio Programs for High-School English." *The English Journal* 28.10 (1939): 835–839.

Dr. Ginsberg explores the programs for using general broadcasts and the prerecorded programs made exclusively for classroom use. He makes a list of programs and guides for students to listen to outside and inside the classroom.

Ginsberg, Walter. "Films for High School English." *The English Journal* 29.1 (1940): 44–49.

Much like his radio drama article, Dr. Ginsberg makes suggestions of movies for students to see that can be valuable in the English classroom.

Reid, Seerely. "Hollywood Hokum—The English Teacher's Responsibility." *The English Journal* 29.3 (1940): 211–218.

Seerely Reid's article argues that teachers must train students to be "movie choosers" instead of moviegoers. To achieve this end, the article states that teachers should spend the first month of English class teaching students to be an informed and discriminating audience of motion pictures.

Ginsberg, Walter. "How Helpful are Shakespeare Recordings?" *The English Journal* 29.4 (1940): 289–300.

This article reports the findings of an experimental use of phonograph recordings of Shakespeare's plays *Twelfth Night* and *The Merchant of Venice*. Students who participated in the study were reported to have a much greater knowledge and understanding of the material on which they were tested. Walter Ginsberg lists twenty-five positive outcomes from the study.

Tyler, Tracy F. "The Place of the Radio in the Teaching of English." *The English Journal* 29.5 (1940): 394–399.

In this article, Dr. Tyler argues that English classes need to expand their scope and explore the power of communication of the radio. Tyler argues that students spend hours every week dealing with ads, commentary, and narrative on the radio, so the English classroom should expand to include the new medium of radio in its scope, with the hope of developing critical hearers of radio.

Finch, Hardy R. "Motion-Picture Activities in the High School." *The English Journal* 29.6 (1940): 465–470.

Mr. Finch describes the ways in which a school could start a film studies class on campus, along with pedagogical tips and writing assignments he has used in his classes. He notes that by 1940 film use in the classroom is no longer an experiment, but an accepted practice.

Lillard, Richard G. "Movies Aren't Literary." *The English Journal* 29.9 (1940): 735–743.

Richard G. Lillard argues that movies use a visual medium made up of pictures instead of words, so movies cannot be labeled as literary. He states that movies are the "little sister" to literature and should be content with what it does, but it should not aspire to literary art.

Helfer, Katherine, and Regina Rosiny. "The Film in the English Class." *The English Journal* 30.1 (1941): 68–71.

This short article runs counter to Richard G. Lillard's argument. Katherine Helfer and Regina Rosiny contend that movies are animated English texts. They argue that movies (called photoplays in the article) can be used to discuss plot, characterization, mood, etc., and they have intrinsic value.

Rishworth, Thomas D. "Responsibility of the School in Educational Broadcasting." *The English Journal* 30.4 (1941): 287–293.

In this article, Thomas D. Rishworth points out that educational broadcasting is ineffective on several levels because it only reaches the already educated. There is a huge disconnect in educational radio broadcasts to the underachieving populace. The article speculates on reasons why this disconnect occurs, and what can be done to improve the situation.

Bonawit, Dorothy. "Motion-Picture Syllabus." *The English Journal* 31.5 (1942): 392–399.

Dorothy Bonawit's article is a rationale and syllabus for film study in a junior level classroom in a typical American high school. She offers pre- and post-unit assessment and a day-by-day syllabus to follow with aims and goals of each day's activity. The syllabus aims to develop "taste" and expertise in evaluating films.

De Lay, Frank P. "Radio Dramatics as a Teaching Device." *The English Journal* 31.10 (1942): 713–719.

This fascinating article talks about how to set up a school radio production on a very limited budget. Frank P. De Lay explains exactly the costs and equipment needed to put on a very pedestrian production. He points out that students can learn a lot from transforming literature into radio drama, even in poorer school districts.

Gilburt, Samuel G. "Radio Appreciation: A Plea and a Program." *The English Journal* 32.8 (1943): 431–435.

Samuel G. Gilburt begins the article by telling several stories of the power of radio. He then argues that students need to be informed about this powerful media and its influence. He concludes his piece with a quick course outline to teach radio appreciation.

Miller, Nathan R. "Using the Recorder in Oral Remedial Reading." *The English Journal* 32.9 (1943): 510–511.

In this short essay, Nathan R. Miller explains his use of the recorder to help remedial students with recognition, pronunciation, etc. Miller states that he has had success in using this technique in the junior high classroom.

Novotny, Lillian. "NCTE Radio Awards Program." *The English Journal* 35.3 (1946): 149–152.

Perhaps hidden by the title, the NCTE Radio Awards project is actually a classroom criterion-based writing lesson. Students are given a standardized evaluation sheet and asked to critically analyze radio programs in order to find the best ones. The assignment stresses critical evaluation of the medium.

Brown, Corinne B. "Teaching Spelling with a Tachistoscope." *The English Journal* 40.2 (1951): 104–105.

This interesting article suggests that using a tachistoscope can help with vocabulary drills in the English classroom. The tachistoscope functions as a slide projector that blocks the slide after a few seconds. It was originally used by pilots and gunners during the war to develop sight recognition of planes so they would only fire on the enemy.

Anker, Lieber. "Television, Here I Come." *The English Journal* 40.4 (1951): 218–220.

Lieber Anker reports on a survey he conducted of sophomores and their viewing habits. Originally, Anker argued against students watching television; however, after surveying his students, he softens his view and suggests ways television could be adapted.

Boutwell, William D. "What We Can Do about Movies, Radio, and Television." *The English Journal* 41.3 (1952): 131–136.

Mr. Boutwell delves into the arguments surrounding the use of modern technology in the classroom. He posits several questions and answers to common arguments in the case. He ends the article with a list of policy changes the United States can make to ensure decent use of this technology in the classroom.

Roody, Sarah I. "Effect of Radio, Television, and Motion Picture on the Development of Maturity." *The English Journal* 41.5 (1952): 245–250.

Sarah I. Roody's article argues that English classrooms have a special responsibility to teach students to become sophisticated listeners and viewers of this new technology. She lists ways in which students can scaffold up to more discriminating consumers.

Thomas, Cleveland. "Recent Audio-Visual Aids in Secondary-School English." *The English Journal* 41.6 (1952): 313–317.

This annotated bibliography lists many interesting articles on audio-visual technology in the classroom. Most of the articles referenced are from now defunct magazines and journals.

Stengel, Stuart. "What Is the High School Teacher of English Doing about Television?" *The English Journal* 43.3 (1954): 120–124.

This article looks at some of the fundamental questions that are asked about television and English studies; however, Stuart Stengel identifies an interesting point of questioning. He submits that TV bombards viewers with so much information that there is little or no time for self-reflected digestion of the content. He concludes that we must encourage deeper viewing by students.

Whittaker, Charlotte C. "Television and a Senior Literature Program." *The English Journal* 43.4 (1954): 183–186.

Charlotte C. Whittaker contends that since most students have television sets in their homes, why not use mass culture to bridge students' lives to great literature. She uses several examples, including connecting WWII documentaries seen on TV with novels such as Herman Wouk's *The Caine Mutiny.*

Thorton, Helen. "A-V Education for Non-Academics." *The English Journal* 43.9 (1954): 512–515.

This article explores the idea of teaching critical evaluation skills for students who view the high school diploma as a terminal degree. Helen Thorton contends that students who carry on with their scholarship have more opportunities to become critical viewers, but those on the terminal graduation track must become better viewers since this is their only chance to develop those skills.

Forsdale, Louis, and Alice Sterner. "A Television Award." *The English Journal* 43.9 (1954): 520–521.

Louis Forsdale and Alice Sterner explain that the NCTE is giving an award for the best educational television program. They then go over the criteria and rationale for the award.

Muri, John T. "The Use of Recordings in High School English Classes." *The English Journal* 46.1 (1957): 32–39.

In this article, Chairman Muri summarizes the findings of the NCTE's Committee on Recordings survey given to high school English teachers. The findings show which recordings were considered most beneficial for the classroom.

Kaplan, Milton A. "Television Drama: A Discussion." *The English Journal* 47.9 (1958): 549–561.

Written in discussion format, this article brings together teachers and people in the television industry to discuss the points of agreement and contention in television as an educational medium. They do not come to many consensus points, but the discussion is frank and interesting.

Brunstein, James J. "Ten Uses for Commercial Television in the English Classroom." *The English Journal* 47.9 (1958): 566–569.

James J. Brunstein adopts the tried and true method of a top ten list as a springboard to discuss television use in the classroom. He offers some fun teaching tips, such as making mock TV shows, adopting game show formats for studying, and making "live" broadcasts. While the list is informative, nothing on the list is particularly new in the scope of the journal.

Hazard, Patrick D., and Mary Hazard. "The Public Arts: 'What's TV Doing to English?'" *The English Journal* 48.7 (1959): 414–416.

This article looks at television and English studies in a slightly different way. In effect, Patrick D. Hazard and Mary Hazard argue that teachers could shift their teaching to match what's on TV. If westerns or detective shows are dominating, then teach westerns or detective fiction. This narrative article also functions as a mini literature review of books and journals that deal with mass media and teaching.

Hazard, Patrick D., and Mary Hazard. "The Public Arts: 'What's TV Doing to English? Part II'" *The English Journal* 48.8 (1959): 491–493.

A continuation of the article that appeared in the October issue, Patrick D. Hazard and Mary Hazard explore the cultural battles swirling around the ideas of television in US society. They draw comparisons to technological innovations and cultural currents in England before 1950.

Goldstein, Miriam. "Humanities through Television." *The English Journal* 49.4 (1960): 250–255.

In this article, Miriam Goldstein relates the findings of a pilot program instituted in her school to use television to teach the humanities. She gives the weekly breakdown of the program, and offers her assessment of the teachers' roles and the students' reactions to the program. She concludes with a section looking at the weaknesses of the program. For instance, she says the pilot program was structured in such a way that she had no time for her remedial students.

Noble, Donald. "Television Script Reports." *The English Journal* 49.4 (1960): 259–261.

Donald Noble presents a short teaching idea of writing a script from a classic novel instead of a traditional book report. Student would have to consider props, setting, and characterization.

Steinberg, Erwin R. "Television and the Teaching of English." *The English Journal* 49.7 (1960): 484–485.

Erwin R. Steinberg's essay contends that even cliché-ridden, stereotypical TV trash can be used for academic value by teaching the students to critically analyze the generic plot and character devices used in those shows.

Willens, Anita J. "TV—Lick It or Join It?" *The English Journal* 49.9 (1960): 639–640.

This article reports on an informal experiment conducted on one hundred fourteen year olds. Anita J. Willens asked them a series of survey questions to elicit responses about TV viewing habits. She then spent several weeks attempting to teach critical viewing strategies with them, and then she gave a post-experiment questionnaire to see if the student viewership had changed. She believes it had.

Hoth, William E. "From Skinner to Crowder to Chance: A Primer on Teaching Machines." *The English Journal* 50.6 (1961): 398–401.

William E. Hoth's article looks at teaching machines based on the theories of B. F. Skinner and N. A. Crowder. He argues that in the future teaching machines might help teachers with grading and learning in the classroom. The examples he uses are basic knowledge and comprehension- type questions. He doesn't mention any composing assignments, but he does mention how useful these machines would be in helping with sentence diagramming.

Lumsden, Robert. "Dictation Machines as Teacher Aids." *The English Journal* 50.8 (1961): 555–556.

This essay argues that using dictation machines to respond to papers will speed up the process and save the teacher time. Once the instructor has marked grammatical corrections, he responds to each paper in a dictation machine. The following day the teacher brings the dictation disc to school and gives it to a stenographer to type up and then give to the students.

Nevi, Charles N., and Lloyd Hoffine. "We Can't Ignore the Mass Media." *The English Journal* 51.8 (1962): 560–564.

In this article, Charles N. Nevi and Lloyd Hoffine argue that all English courses should include a unit on evaluating and analyzing the mass media. While a majority of the article deals with television and its application to literature, they also include a section on newspapers and magazines in the classroom as well.

Erwin, Gloria. "The Overhead Projector-Aid to the Composition Program." *The English Journal* 53.1 (1964): 48–50.

Gloria Erwin argues that her class has benefited from the use of an overhead projector in her composition class. She uses the overhead to teach proper punctuation, structure, and transitioning, and she uses it to critique student papers. She states that her students' writing has improved since she began using the overhead projector.

Sheely, Stuart L. "Tape Recorders and Writing: Innovation in Indianapolis." *The English Journal* 57.5 (1968): 637–640.

This article relates a project undertaken by the Indianapolis public high school system to have students writing essays compose with the help of a reel-to-reel tape recorder. Students can stop and start the recorder with a pedal, and they can compose orally to help them with their writing. The project has the underlying assumption that speech is primary and only with oral help can students compose effectively.

Glennon, Michael L. "Small Groups and Short Films." *The English Journal* 57.5 (1968): 641–645.

In this essay Michael L. Glennon shares a new technique he uses with students in his film class. He schedules student seminars only in groups of ten or fewer and meets with them only once a week. The other times the students meet with their group to discuss projects. He has multiple groups running at the same time, but he makes the learning very student-centered. He also offers eleven points to help teachers thinking about implementing this seminar make the transition.

Stern, Adele H. "Using Films in Teaching English Composition." *The English Journal* 57.5 (1968): 646–649.

Since written composition is often concerned with form and function, Adele H. Stern addresses the ideas of translating these concepts into movie viewing. She argues that by teaching students to read a movie, and then they will be able to take those skills from the classroom, but also use those skills to improve the reading of literature.

O'Connor, Marie E. "The Research Paper and the Tape Recorder." *The English Journal* 57.5 (1968): 652–653+ 660.

Marie E. O'Connor explains her creative use of the tape recorder for completing the research assignment in her courses. Instead of having the typical dry research assignment, she has the students turn their research into a ten-minute radio broadcast. Since the broadcasts are fairly long, the teacher only has five or six due a week, creating less grading per week.

Brandon, Liane. "Using Media Creatively in the English Classroom." *The English Journal* 60.9 (1971): 1231–1233.

This short pedagogical article lists several project ideas for using media in the classroom. Liane Brandon offers project ideas for photography, recordings, film, and television.

Danielson, Earl R., Lesley A. Burrows, and David A. Rosenberg. "The Cassette Tape: An Aid to Individualizing High School English." *The English Journal* 62.3 (1973): 441–445.

In this article, Earl R. Danielson, Lesley A. Burrows, and David A. Rosenberg grapple with the idea of trying to reach all of their students adequately when they are in classrooms with a 30:1 student teacher ratio. Their contention is that by making audio books available to students, they can individualize the leaning experience of each student based on their developmental level, and thus improve the quality of education.

Morrow, James, and Murray Suid. "Media in the English Classroom: Some Pedagogical Issues." *The English Journal* 63.7 (1974): 37–44.

There are two major elements to point out here. First, in 1974, *English Journal* went from a continuously paginated journal to an individually paginated journal. Second, the 63.7 volume of *EJ* had a theme of technology. There are many articles in this particular edition that deal with technology. That said, this article examines the pedagogical issues of media in the classroom. James Morrow and Murray Suid argue that the problems with print media versus visual media are overblown. They can be very complimentary. They also argue that the current trend to value process over product can be somewhat mitigated by looking at films where the product is the important part, not the process of making the film.

Speier, Sandra. "The Commercial 8mm Film: Classroom Pizzazz at Bargain Rates." *English Journal* 63.7 (1974): 81–82.

Sandra Speier examines the use of 8mm films in the classroom noting that these films are beneficial for several reasons, especially in price, selection, and application. She also explores the use of these films in a unit curriculum.

Morrow, James. "Media Literacy in the 80s." *The English Journal* 69.1 (1980): 48–51.

This critical essay criticizes the concept of technological determinism and suggests that in the 1980s the critical viewer will see the transformative power of media in the classroom regardless of medium. Finally, in some ways, James Morrow is asking teachers and students to view media critically, yet embrace all media—even rather old-fashioned media, like radio drama and slide shows.

Freed, Peggy. "Writing with the Opaque Projector." *English Journal* 70.2 (1981): 31–33.

In this article, Peggy Freed discusses the use of an opaque projector, which can project the page of a book or a student paper onto the classroom screen. While she argues that projecting student papers onto the screen will help organization, audience, and purpose, a large majority of the article is looking at basic surface-level issues, like punctuation and grammar.

Bily, Mark J., et al. "Our Readers Write: What Is the Most Successful Way I Ever Used AV Material or Equipment?" *English Journal* 70.7 (1981): 78–82.

This article is a conglomeration of short anecdotes by educators on their most successful uses of AV equipment in the classroom. Some are quite ingenious; others are commonsense uses of technology available in the 1980s.

White, Gene. "From Magic Lanterns to Microcomputers: The Evolution of the Visual Aid in the English Classroom." *English Journal* 73.3 (1984): 59–62.

Gene White has compiled a short history of audio-visual material for use specifically in the English classroom. He cites several older articles in *EJ*, and he traces the currents and trends of these emerging technologies in the classroom. Perhaps this article is important since it teeters on the brink of digital domination in the schools. He offers a look back before teachers step into the future.

Farmer, David L. "The VCR: Raiders as a Teaching Tool." *English Journal* 76.1 (1987): 31.

This very short article details the use of VCRs, specifically how this new technology can easily be used in English classrooms. His example is teaching *Indiana Jones: The Raiders of the Lost Ark*. He compares this new, effective, inexpensive technology to Shakespeare's acting troupe for entertainment.

JAC

JAC is mostly a theory-based journal. We have found in our research for this annotated bibliography that the more theoretical the journals become, the fewer pre-computer technology issues are advanced in the journal's discourse. It is not surprising then to find only a few pre-computer technology articles in the pages of *JAC*.

Medlicott, Jr., Alexander. "Cassette Commentary: An Approach to the Teaching of Expository Writing." *JAC* 1.1 (1980). Web. 28 July 2011.

In this essay, Alexander Medlicott, Jr. explains his use of cassette comments in his composition classroom. He contends that in this multimedia culture, students will listen to the comments and spare the teacher from "the exhausting ordeal of extensive written comments." He claims the cassette tapes these days are small, reliable, and effective for use in the classroom.

Pelz, Karen. "A Reply to Medlicott: Evaluating Writing." *JAC* 1.1 (1980). Web. 28 July 2011.

In this response to Alexander Medlicott, Jr.'s article, Karen Pelz offers a rather scathing indictment against cassette commentary. She contends that the lack of positive written models has weakened student writing skills. She notes that we must communicate out values to our students by responding in ways that will show we read and value their expression.

Jobst, Jack. "The Technical Talk: More Effective Use of Visual Aids." *JAC* 2.1 (1981). Web. 28 July 2011.

Jack Jobst contends that while students are being asked to produce more and more visual and technical presentation material, they are offered very few examples of how to do it effectively. This article looks at a seminar Jobst attended, and where he realized his lack of skills in technology. He presents a simple way students can use 35mm slides effectively in class presentations using a slide projector.

Welch, Kathleen. "Electrifying Classical Rhetoric: Ancient Media, Modern Technology, and Contemporary Composition." *JAC* 10.1 (1990). Web. 28 July 2011.

This very interesting article looks at electronic discourse as secondary orality. Kathleen Welch considers the Greek technology of the day, as well as the delivery medium, and compares that to the electronic delivery we have today. She contends that a lot of our definitions, such as audience, may have to evolve to encompass the newer technologies, but since rhetoric is adaptable, she doesn't feel there is need to panic.

RHETORIC REVIEW

Being a historical and theoretical journal, *Rhetoric Review* did not have much regarding technology in relation to rhetoric within the scope of this project. There is a theme among many articles, however, that rhetorical study and applications cannot be regulated to certain genres or communication mediums. The article represented here illustrates one technology highlighted for more study.

Wicks, Ulrich. "Studying Film as Integrated Text." *Rhetoric Review* 2.1 (1983): 51–62.

Ulrich Wicks argues for a deeper and more constructed analysis of film in the composition/rhetoric classroom considering not only implications of television and film on society, but the historical implications as well. This article examines the broad constructs film has to offer to a large societal base and how the prophecies of George Orwell and Plato, which foresee a society overrun by lingo and quick speak, might come to fruition should film be left unstudied and without criticism.

Written Communications

Because *Written Communications* published its first issue in 1984, the technology mentioned is predominantly the computer or computer-related developments. Particularly since the 1990s, technology in written communication has become a major focus of the journal. While the use of noncomputer technologies is occasionally implied in the earlier issues, it is seldom mentioned or discussed explicitly. (For example, protocol analysis is a common methodology in the mid and late 1980s, but the use of recording devices is by then so commonly accepted that it does not merit explanation or discussion.) In a review of the issue from the journal's inception through 2008, the most relevant articles were both by Elizabeth Tebeaux, who contributed historical treatments of how advancements in technology furthered the technical writing of the English Renaissance.

Tebeaux, Elizabeth. "Technical Writing for Women of the English Renaissance: Technology, Literacy, and the Emergence of a Genre." *Written Communication* 10.2 (1993): 164–199.

Little known how-to books provide valuable insight into the technologies used by women of the English Renaissance. Advancements in print technology coincided with the demise in emphasis on oral discourse and resulted in the rise of technical writing in its most popular form, directed to women and providing instruction in gardening, cooking, needlecraft, home remedies, midwifery, and other homemaking skills. Women's maturing literacy at that time is inextricably linked to the development of the technical writing genre and the increased accessibility it provided.

Tebeaux, Elizabeth. "Ramus, Visual Rhetoric, and the Emergence of Page Design in Medical Writing of the English Renaissance: Tracking the Evolution of Readable Documents." *Written Communication* 8.4 (1991): 411–445.

Elizabeth Tebeaux proposes that the influence of Ramist logic combined with advances in print technology resulted in the improvement of textual design in technical "how-to" manuals in Renaissance England, particularly medical manuals. Deliberate and logical spatial arrangement of components, including the use of tables, brackets, and enumerated summaries, contributed to increased readability. The rhetorical power of typography realized by improved page design fostered a change in sensibility whereby the modern regard of the textbook as a both accessible and reliable reference came into being.

9 The Rhetoric of Obfuscation and Technologies of Hidden Writing: Poets and Palimpsests, Painters and Purposes

Jason Thompson and Theresa Enos

Though *palimpsest* combines the words for "rubbed smooth" and "again," the *OED* suggests *palimpsest* carries within it the connotation of recantation: the word *palinodia* (combination of "sing" and "again") refers to lyric poet Stesichorus, who, having gone blind after attacking Helen, "received [his sight back] only after making a recantation of what he had said" (Lempriere 645). That "again" suggests a purposeful action—once done, we seldom rewrite or revise without cause. Stesichorus sought to undo the damage he had incurred by singing—what kind of damage has been done by writing, and how have we sought to undo it? How also have we damaged innocent writing by undoing it? Put another way, what happens when we see the page, or the words on the page, or the ethos evoked by the words, as a code?

We are now familiar with the word *palimpsest* as an early form of recycling, a parchment or tablet in the form of a codex—a manuscript—that has been erased and rewritten and that still shows traces of its earlier form. The Archimedes Palimpsest is the best-known example. Discovered in 1899, the overlapped writings on the codex are the works of Archimedes, the ancient Greek mathematician, engineer, and philosopher (287?–212 BCE). In the twelfth century, this parchment was scraped so that the earlier writing was mostly erased but still legible, and Christian texts were written at right angles on top of the earlier text. Archimedes's work, however, was not the only text recycled into the palimpsest: it contains pages from no less than four other sources ("The Palimpsest").[1]

The Romans had come up with another form of palimpsest; instead of scraping vellum parchment, they made wooden tablets covered with wax so the wax surface could be smoothed out after each writing and reused. (We get the term *clean slate*, of course, from the Latin *tabula rasa*.) Still, earlier traces of writing could be discerned on this kind of codex, too. The idea of a codex or earlier text that has been "written over" was further extended in the eighteenth century as a paper or parchment used for making a first draft, which could then be erased and a revised text written over the original.

The term has become a metaphor for an object or image that reveals its history, anything that has diverse layers or aspects apparent beneath its surface. Thomas De Quincey in his *Suspira de Profundis* asks: "What else than a natural and mighty palimpsest is the human brain?" And George Orwell in *1984* said that "[a]ll history is a palimpsest, scraped clean and reinscribed exactly as often as was necessary" (40). We can further use palimpsest as metaphor by recognizing that besides being any object with multiple layers, a place or area that reflects its history can be seen as a palimpsest. John McPhee spoke of sixteenth-century Spaniards in the New World who "saw an ocean moving south . . . through a palimpsest of bayous and distributary streams in forested paludal basins" (qtd. in Dearborn xx).

To Walter Henry, creator of CoOL databases, a palimpsest is "an analog of all texts, which carry with them the traces of their past, their dialogue with past texts, with the history of language," thus "the palpable, deducible mystery." To Henry the word *palimpsest* is the right word to call a digital environment, "whose contents are overwritten continually, sometimes even continuously, one layer overlaying the next, over, and over."

The term *palimpsest* referring to a surface that has been written upon several times can be linked to ethos, a layering of texts and/or voices that can reveal our persona, character, hidden intention. Our studies of ethos throughout history have shown that the author's attempt at creating an image of how he or she wants to be perceived—the coding of intention—oftentimes invites the corresponding readerly desire to decode that intention and thus solve the mystery. Authors have deliberately employed what we call "the rhetoric of obfuscation"—a sort of Hitchcockian MacGuffin—in order to misdirect readers. We argue here not for the decoding of such rhetorics but for their untouched consideration, a difficult though rewarding process John Keats called "negative capability." Indeed, examples from the art world prove suggestive: artists are allowed to struggle with contradiction in a way composition students frequently are not. We maintain the value in the paradoxical embrace of ambiguity and see in it a possible readerly *techne*, in addition to a viable writing pedagogy that asks us to see our students, at least in part, as artists.

This essay explores connections among various "rhetorics of obfuscation" (the Archimedes Palimpsest, Da Vinci's notebooks, and others) in order to explore them as instructive writing technologies in use long before the computer. We use the palimpsest as a metaphor for rhetorics of obfuscation, which enables us then to argue for a kairotic ethos to make what appears to be the invisible reveal itself through the text. First, we situate and define palimpsest historically and metaphorically. Next, we turn to Plato for a view of ambiguity that contrasts the multiplicity of the palimpsest. To get us closer to rhetorics of obfuscation through misdirection, we discuss Da Vinci's notebooks and the movie *The Da Vinci Code*. Then, we move on to another form of hidden writing, invisible writing, by way of both a narrative about writing and some composition research from the 1970s. Finally, we suggest implications of rhetorics of obfuscation: kairotic ethos.

PLATO, NONCONTRADICTION, AND THE DISQUIETING NATURE OF AMBIGUITY

There are serious impediments to seeing our history, our places, our writing, our ethos, our students, and our minds in this way, as palimpsests whose mysteries should be maintained and explored, not solved and thereby destroyed. Standing in stark opposition to the dynamism and heuristic multiplicity of the palimpsest is Plato, whose law of noncontradiction haunts us even now, with its implicit argument against ambiguity, with its insistence that any given thing must be only itself.

Beginning with him (and probably earlier than that), the law of noncontradiction finds its earliest expression from the character of Socrates, speaking in the *Republic*. Socrates imparts to Glaucon how social justice, in an ideal society, occurs when the three classes of people—producers, auxiliaries, and guardians—effect a harmony of balanced proportion. This social justice mirrors individual justice when the three classes of the soul—rational, spirited, and appetitive—accept the rule of rationality and thus achieve a perfect balance. Amid Socrates's lesson he articulates the law that would allow for such comforting hierarchy: "It is obvious that the same thing will not at one and the same time, in the same part of it, and in the same relation, do two opposite things or be in two opposite states" (436). Otherwise put: the road to Megara can only lead to Megara.

Right after stating the law, Socrates cautions Glaucon by warning him against swift answers. In the least defensible translation of this sentence, Benjamin Jowett puts it: "Still, I said, let us have a more precise statement of terms, lest we should hereafter fall out by the way" ("The Republic, IV"). Jowett interprets the Greek phrase along a travel metaphor. In Paul Shorey's translation he offers it thus: "Let us have our understanding still more precise, lest as we proceed we become involved in dispute"; imprecision will make the journey so bumpy that the speakers will lose themselves (383). This articulation conjures a verbal melee, something unwanted—to avoid the wrangle, precision should be a common guide. In A. D. Lindsay's translation Socrates says, "Let us come to a more exact understanding. If we go too fast we may fall into ambiguities" (117).

Consulting the Greek text, Jason finds the word is *amphisbetesomen*, from *amphobolos*.[2] According to the Liddell Scott entry, *amphibolos* means, first, "encompassing," as in a net.[3] Second, *amphibolos* can translate to "attacked on both sides" or "double-pointed" (as in "hitting on both ends").[4] Last, the word denotes "doubtful" or "ambiguous," and as an extension, "of persons in doubt" ("Amphibolos").[5] Of the three main uses, this sense of "ambiguous" has by far the most examples drawn from classical texts: considering this moment in the *Republic*, it is the definition most helpful and illuminating. The Greek word for *ambiguity* seems to have been employed by extant playwrights to describe anything (usually a noun like *clothes* or *net*) that encircles, specifically, a body or bodies. Historians then expanded *amphobolos* to include a sense of physical attack, specifically the notion of ambush or overwhelming forces attacking from both or all sides. From there it apparently underwent a final shift into abstraction: a double meaning, a doubtful meaning. It is worth noting that in the classical imagination, nearly all instantiations of ambiguity are negative. As noted by John Chamberlin, "Both Aristotelian and Stoic philosophers [. . .] regarded the investigation of ambiguity not as a resource for the exploration of meaning so much as a way of avoiding misunderstanding—i.e., they took a disjunctive approach" (25). It is easy to picture how the discovery of an ambiguity could materialize the law of noncontradiction and not the exploration of meaning, and we are impoverished for it.

Great comfort attends the disambiguation of a particular meaning, a puzzle, a code, a voice, a way; however, as Kenneth Burke warned in his fifth clause of the Definition of Man, we humans are "rotten with perfection": this is Aristotle's "entelechal principle" wherein any given terminology has implications that when carried out, reach their ultimate end (16). This perfection cannot grow and must not change. Put another way, we seek, and in seeking make, and in making force others. We typically strive to know absolutely, and this absolute knowledge rarely benefits our particular communities. Burke asked us—in nearly everything he wrote—to live with the anxiety not of not knowing, and of not needing to know the sure answer all the time. What if literary analysts were heralded not for their narrow and singular vision but instead for the multiplicity of interpretations possible? Poets were barred from Plato's *Republic* because they could offer powerful and ambiguous alternatives to rigid codes, alternatives that would not square with the law of noncontradiction because they could not be solved deductively. What if instead of solving codes, we could live in them?

DA VINCI NOTEBOOKS, *THE DA VINCI CODE*

Although Jean Paul Richter bemoans that the texts should be so long unpublished and so long unread, in the preface to his 1883 *The Notebooks of Leonardo Da Vinci Compiled and Edited from the Original Manuscripts By Jean Paul Richter*, he fully understands the many impediments to their publication.[6] He cites Vasari's characterization of Da Vinci's unique writing style: "[H]e wrote backwards, in rude characters, and with the left hand, so that any one who is not practiced in reading them, cannot understand them" (qtd. in Richter xiv). In addition, Richter goes on to catalogue, in a nine-page prolegomena, further textual intricacies, including clerical errors, misspellings, abbreviations, symbols, compound formations, and different text colors (1–9). What's more, Da Vinci completely omits accents and apostrophes; he does away with all conventional punctuation (comma, period, colon, semicolon, exclamation point, question mark). All of this textual evidence—over five thousand manuscript pages—suggests that Da Vinci intentionally made his notebooks inscrutable, though as Richter points out, the notebooks also contain many references to arrangement of the books. Clearly, Da Vinci wanted the notebooks to be published, but why would he write in code? This is a natural question, but it is the wrong one to ask because it makes the notebooks into a puzzle to be solved, which takes us back to Plato and noncontradiction, the inevitable spiral into the kind of entrenchment that characterizes much of modern scholarship. A better question: how did Da Vinci make connections among disparate items? What if you had a book outlining thirty years of such connections that you recorded daily during your own life, would you agree that the book must ultimately mean one thing? Would it not seem reductive and comical to hear how a scholar had decoded the meaning of your various coded days, had extrapolated the implied premises from the enthymematic record of your life?

Just this has been occurring in notebook scholarship. Da Vinci scholar Robert Zwijnenberg outlines its history and finds its modern beginning in 1880, with specialists like Seailles, Muntz, and Solmi concentrating on the science of Da Vinci by "reading past" the fragmentation of the notes and "solving" the problem of their chaos. This scholarship underwent a shift away from science and toward his art, and finally toward his thinking as represented on the page (5–7). In one famous case study, no less a luminary than Dr. Sigmund Freud applied his theory of psychoanalysis on Da Vinci's personality, centered in part on the notebooks. Based on an early "fantasy about a vulture, the nature and composition of his paintings, and slips and errors found in his writing," Freud concluded that Da Vinci "had the characteristics of a neurotic obsessional personality" (qtd. in Aaron and Clouse 1). P. G. Aaron and Robert G. Clouse argue that Freud's diagnosis was incorrect and explain that the disorder of the notebooks may be explained by "recent neuropsychological investigations" that show how the human brain develops two separate modes of processing information, and these modes correspond to clear-cut left-hemisphere/right-hemisphere specialization (4–5). Da Vinci's brain, they argue, had a "diffuse organization": in other words, Da Vinci's notebooks are the record of a mind talking to itself in its own language. Recall De Quincey: "What else than a natural and mighty palimpsest is the human brain?"

Zwijnenberg agrees, but begins his treatise on the notebooks by considering them rhetorically, as products of a humanist education. After reviewing the history of rhetoric (by following the familiar Cicero-Quintilian path from antiquity to the Renaissance), Zwijnenberg makes the case for "the notebook technique" of storing memory coming from Quintilian's *Institutio Oratoria*, particularly his *progymnasmata* (14). He cites Agricola's quotation that "knowledge is worthless unless one has it at one's fingertips" and Alberti's injunction to keep such notebooks (15). Lastly, the author makes the case that for Da Vinci the notebooks offered up a universe of visual loci. In other words, over a lifetime of stutter-stops and unrealized projects, Da Vinci understood and used his notebooks every day; they allowed him to make sense of the world by bookmarking, in a significant way, his memory. To read the notebooks in this way—generously, openly, and alive to their possibility—asks the reader to cultivate what the humanists called *ingenium*: that ability to make connections between things, as Da Vinci himself must have done in order to write the notebooks. *Ingenium* is no lost art, but it is an art that wants practice.

Most recently, the aura of Da Vinci's mastermind code-world has been illuminated and increased by Dan Brown's 2003 bestseller *The Da Vinci Code*, which has sold seventy million copies worldwide and has been adapted into a Hollywood movie that grossed $757 million dollars in the worldwide box office, making it the twenty-second highest-grossing film of all time. The novel makes many oblique references to the codes contained in Da Vinci's paintings; it also is about ancient secret societies, modern forensics, science and engineering, and the history of religion. The basic thesis is that Da Vinci was a member of a secret society charged with protecting the true history of Christianity until the world is ready to hear it.

Entrusting a messenger with private communication always has been problematic; after all, the messenger might be paid more to sell the information than to deliver as promised. So, Brown tells us in the novel, Da Vinci centuries ago invented a rudimentary form of public-key encryption: "a portable container to safeguard documents," which is a tube with lettered dials:

> The dials have to be rotated to a proper sequence, spelling out the password, for the cylinder to slide apart. Once a message was "encrypted" inside the container only an individual with the correct password could open it. This encryption method

was physically unhackable: If anyone tried to force the container open, the information inside would self-destruct. Da Vinci rigged this by writing his message on a papyrus scroll and rolling it around a delicate glass vial filled with vinegar. If someone attempted to force the container open, the vial would break, and the vinegar would dissolve the papyrus almost instantly. (Delio)

Brown also brings readers into the Cathedral of Codes, a chapel in Great Britain, with a "ceiling from which hundreds of stone blocks protrude [. . .] [each] carved with a symbol that, when combined, is thought to create the world's largest cipher" (Delio).

In the novel, a professor of Religious Symbology solves a murder mystery through his decoding of several of Da Vinci's most iconographic images: *The Vitruvian Man*, *The Mona Lisa*, and *The Last Supper*. The book is brilliant in its exploration of cryptology, particularly the encoding methods developed by Da Vinci, whose "art and manuscripts are packed with mystifying symbolism and quirky codes" (Delio). Indeed, the book most of all is about the history of encryption and the many methods developed over time to keep private information from prying eyes. It is sufficient to observe that the book sparked international debate on the correctness of its interpretation. Titles like *Da Vinci Code Decoded* and *Truth and Fiction in the Da Vinci Code* promise that "expert historians," Martin Lunn and Bart A. Ehrman, respectively, will clear the ambiguities brought about by Brown's novel. The discourse surrounding the *Da Vinci Code* would have made Plato's Socrates proud—Da Vinci, despite ample textual evidence to the contrary, could not "do two opposite things" and was systematically "perfected" by alternate camps in a flurry of discourse that Burke might have named the War of Nerves.

MAKING THE INVISIBLE VISIBLE: INVENTION, ETHOS, TIME, AND SPACE

The blank page frightens
. . . .
The blank page without expression
threatens to take yours.
It wants part of you.
. . . .

> *You have nothing more to say.*
> *The blank page is full. It has won.*

> —Becke Roughton, "Power of the Blank Page"

"We must pile time into [. . .] discourse," Jim Corder reminds us again and again in his many essays calling for us to foreground invention and ethos in our writing classes, "to help us make sense of a world that doesn't want time in its discourses." ("Argument" 31)

Building a spacious rhetoric that enabled him to construct a public self that would be seen as continuous with the private is what occupied Corder in his life's work. He wasn't interested in completely finishing that process or in fully articulating a new rhetoric. This is why the canon of Invention is paramount in his rhetoric: resistance to closure, embrace of ambiguity, and a recursive process of coding and decoding that strives for open-endedness.

Corder's ideas on ethos—in particular, generative ethos—help show us how we can build public selves to make our private selves transparent. Thus palimpsest closely links to ethos: a layering of voices that can be decoded to reveal our persona, character, intention. Seeking to understand, even reveal, the ethos residing under the text is one way of seeing how the rhetoric of obfuscation works, seeing the subtext under a layer of text, uncovering voice, hidden intention, character. Corder's style in nearly any of his essays, where he masterfully melds the personal with the academic, is a lesson in persuading through apparent obfuscation. The openings of most of his essays misdirect us, or so we might think, until we realize how he makes his point stronger, even if sometimes indirectly, by taking us through a maze of code-like metaphors where he is able to pile time and build space. We need time and space first of all, Corder tells us, and it is generative ethos that embodies the process of making itself and of liberating hearers to make themselves. In this form of ethos, there is "always more coming. It is never over, never wholly fenced into the past." Its layers, upon close scrutiny, are transparent one to the other, and are a "speaking out from history onto history" ("Varieties" 14).

Generative ethos as a transforming power allows us to hear another other than only ourselves, to see layers of text and meaning: "We may hear ourselves," Corder says, "not another; the other's words may act only as a trigger to release our own, unlocking not the other's mean-

ing, but one we already possessed." When this happens, "we are bound
in space, caught tightly in our own province" ("Varieties" 20).

To Corder, building time and space—seeing discourse as palimpsest—means that we habitually dwell in the inventive universe, in
between layers of text, in that interstitial world. Building time and
space necessitates an open embrace of ambiguity that soundly contests
Plato's law of noncontradiction: one thing can and must be more than
only itself. One thing—one text, one voice, one ethos—must be two
things. To hold the layers of text open is to feel the discomfiture of ir-
resolution: to hold them open is to resist their perfected completion,
and this artistic ability we must perform if we are to make connections, to practice the *ingenium* we have somehow forgotten.

At home Theresa had so many distractions, delaying tactics, of course,
like feeding the birds, watering plants, cleaning the bathroom, that she
found it hard to write. Yet to the amusement of friends and, no doubt,
readers of a little essay she published in *Writers on Writing*, she found
she could write while driving because encapsulated in her car, she was
freed to explore, to invent, to mentally take all kinds of routes seemingly not converging. For years she did her exploratory writing in the
car while driving, where she couldn't walk away to find distractions.
Her practice of hidden writing began when she started teaching (her
first faculty position) at a Dallas university fifty miles from her home
in Fort Worth. Those two hours a day for the two-way trip generated
many of her ideas for teaching writing, for essays that were eventually
published, even for launching *Rhetoric Review*. At first she tried a cassette recorder so she wouldn't lose thoughts coming as fast as the miles
going beneath her, but Theresa is one of those writers who experience
difficulty in "seeing" a concept unless it's written down. Then during
this productive driving time, she tried jotting down key words and
phrases on a note pad, trying to think out a draft and then writing it
from memory later. Nothing worked but actually writing while she
drove. The mechanics were neither difficult nor dangerous. She kept
a yellow pad in her lap or on the center console. She didn't write constantly but in spurts and chunks as her mind traveled and explored,
explored and traveled. With power steering, cruise control, and the
triangular-spoked steering wheel, maintaining control was easy (she
was fortunate to be able to drive to and from her teaching job on an

eight-lane interstate—and not during rush traffic). She insists she *did* drive safely, seldom taking her eyes off the road unfolding in front of her.

She didn't need to see the words unfolding beneath her pen. This discovery draft became necessary for her when she began the painful revision process sitting at home in front of the computer and coaxing out still-hidden ideas behind the partial codex. What Theresa discovered was that not watching herself write this discovery draft, not watching the words and phrases as they tunnel through channels of both mind and pen, allowed her to continue exploring as she drove forward—not so likely to stop in the middle of a sentence to change a word or some phrasing. In the enclosed space of the car, not staring at the blank page, that blank space to be filled, she was free to travel, thought rapidly generating thought as she traveled in both senses. What she found was what she thought was hidden on her own kind of palimpsest.

In the heady revolutionary days of the 1970s and throughout most of the 1980s, rhetoric in its vigorous revival not only marched hand in hand with the process movement but also ensconced itself as the very core of the college writing course. There's so much yet to be done in the historicizing of this era. The various strands, however, are still tenuously entangled: classical rhetoric, the New Rhetoric, composition (not yet Composition Studies), expressionism (the name others gave to those who illuminated the personal, which was already there in all writing in any case), cognitive writing. What tied all these strands together was the focus on invention (whether called invention or prewriting or heuristics or protocols). A little later in this process movement, the recursive quality of invention created acceptance for the notion that associative mental links make manifest the thought coming out of writing and not the product-oriented opposite.

Indeed, invention was a key word in our work with writing in the 1970s and early 1980s. Did it for the most part disappear with the political turn in the 1980s and 1990s, or did it just become so matter of fact and embedded in our theorization of writing that we no longer needed to name the process? Same as the diaspora of style (see Butler).

Little noticed, as far as we've been able to determine, Sheridan Blau wrote on an earlier study of invisible writing conducted by James Britton and expanded that study, with different results. Britton's argument was that rereading, or scanning, parts of what has already been written on the page is an "essential dimension of the cognitive processing that takes place" in most writing tasks (Blau 297). Writers need to scan in order to retain control over their emerging ideas. To test the importance of rereading what has just been written, Britton and three of his colleagues used worn-out ballpoint pens to write so they couldn't see what they had written. They wrote using carbon paper between two pages so they could later read what they had written.[7]

This invisible writing made them uncomfortable because scanning back was impossible—they couldn't reread and revise as they wrote.[8] With narrative they felt less uncomfortable, but they were unable to formulate more theoretical concepts.

Britton was convinced his experiment showed the need for writers to pause in their writing to review what they have written. This rereading allows them to control and direct in a coherent way the direction of their emerging text—and to make corrections as the text develops.

Britton's experiment gave Blau the idea to test cognitive demands that different kinds of discourse make on writers. Using Britton's methodology, Blau also used worn-out pens and carbon paper to obscure student writing. He wanted to further test the need for scanning as "an index of the cognitive difficulty of a task" (298). He asked his group (preservice English education graduate students) to write in modes of increasing difficulty (description, narrative, exploration, exposition, argument, and poetry). He expected the experiment would replicate Britton's, that as his students progressed through the different modes of writing, they would be unable to develop their ideas because they didn't have a visible record of what they were writing.

But Blau's experiment showed that "the absence of visual feedback from the text [his students] were producing actually sharpened their concentration on each of the writing tasks, enhanced their fluency, and yielded texts that were more rather than less cohesive" (Britton, et al. 298).

In the discussion following this experiment, Blau's students said that although the invisible writing neither impeded nor aided their descriptive or narrative writing, in their exposition and argument efforts, they found writing invisible made for more fluent writing: "The invisibility of the words they were writing apparently forced [them] to give more concentrated and sustained attention to their emerging thoughts than they ordinarily gave when working with a working pen or pencil" (299). Rather than their minds wandering after each sentence or two, they could keep their attention on a single train of thought and thus were able to develop more effectively beyond the boundaries of a sentence or two. Invisible writing allowed them to keep their attention on the line of thought they were developing because under the conditions of the experiment, they were unable to edit or rewrite.[9]

Blau's experiments suggest pretty strongly that invisible writing is a powerful aid to first-draft composing.[10] His students' observations about invisible writing are consistent with research on editing: unskilled writers begin editing almost immediately (see Perl, "Understanding Composing"). Beginning to edit at an early stage impedes generative thinking. "Such concentration," Blau says,

> is undoubtedly dissipated when a writer continually interrupts himself by shifting his attention in writing from the thought he is following (or pushing ahead) to the different form of intellectual activity entailed in editing or revising. The distinctive virtue of invisible writing may be that its constraints prevent shifts in attention away from what is essential for a first draft toward what is better postponed to subsequent drafts. (306)

The invisible writing experiments are an interesting part of our history, but they are only a miniscule part of the emphasis on invention that came with the process movement and that shaped the field. There's little if any talk of invention and hasn't been for years (for an exception see Atwill and Lauer). Part of this is that like style and the other canons, invention has been absorbed into our pedagogy so that we don't often see it as a *canon*. Perhaps we should.[11] We're not so foolish as to imagine we can go back to invisible writing. (Carbon paper *is*, however still available—we checked.)

Besides, the revelation of thought through such inventive tactics probably wouldn't work in the classroom: we don't want to be invisible. Indeed, we can't be. We're in a transparent world with blogs and camcorders. Compared to attempts throughout history to hide ourselves through encoded text (palimpsests, notebooks, codes), our striving today to become invisible seems modified by behavior—the fear of being blogged for any slight:

> When everyone has a blog, a MySpace page or Facebook
> entry, everyone is a publisher. When everyone has a cell phone
> with a camera in it, everyone is a paparazzo. When everyone
> can upload video on YouTube, everyone is a filmmaker. When
> everyone is a publisher, paparazzo or filmmaker, everyone is
> a public figure. We're all public figures now. The blogosphere
> has made the global discussion so much richer—and each of
> us so much more transparent. (Friedman)

If invention and style have been absorbed so that we do not see them as
canons, then memory has nearly been obliterated, except of course for
the now commonplace of electronic memory. Indeed, when "memory"
gets referenced today, more often than not the word refers to a hardware component, so necessary to daily operations that one need not
register it as separate from the device it makes possible. Despite its
ubiquity (and thus, seemingly harmlessness), electronic memory may
preclude making ourselves, or anything else, invisible: "The persistence of memory in electronic form makes second chances harder to
come by," writes Seidman. "In the information age, life has no chapters or closets; you can leave nothing behind, and you have nowhere to
hide your skeletons. Your past is your present" (17).

If Seidman is correct, then the information age in its harsh literal-
ism must eschew ambiguity: one thing must be only itself. What is
more, the past in ruthlessly documenting experience determines the
present. In a world where the past is the same as the present—in a
world robbed of the here-and-now—we need more than ever to heed
Corder's injunction to pile time and build space, to make an ethos that
is "never over, never wholly fenced into the past" ("Varieties" 14).

Conclusion: Toward a Kairotic Ethos

Our essay began as an investigation into technologies of hidden writing: we started with the idea of investigating Native American code-
breakers, invisible inks, automatic writing, and the like. We quickly
discovered the resultant essay would take us away from writing as
it is taught and practiced—the process—and toward writing as it is
rendered and guarded—the product. Our focus shifted to interrogate
specific types of hidden writing—Da Vinci's notebooks and hidden
writing—for their rhetorics of obfuscation, and this exploration yielded the present essay, which posits first a way of seeing (the palimp-

sest), next a way of reading (the embrace of ambiguity), and last a way of writing (*ingenium* and Corder's generative ethos). But how does one accomplish this process? We propose the notion of kairos can be synthesized with Corder's generative ethos in order to make manifest kairotic ethos.

In *Ancient Rhetorics for Contemporary Students*, Sharon Crowley and Debra Hawhee articulate connections among Cicero's notion of propriety, the Greek notion of *kairos*, and a writer's style. For Cicero, paramount to successful rhetoric is propriety, which is "what is fitting and agreeable to an occasion or person; it is important often in actions as well as in words, in the expression of the face, in gestures and in gait" (233). The authors link this notion to *kairos*, which they define as "the right or opportune time to write or speak": "Cicero favored a situational propriety, one that comes closer to [. . .] *kairos*" (233). Though it expands to include the overall notion of rhetorical effectiveness, the discussion is limited to a writer's style (as in the third canon).

Jim Corder's "Varieties of Ethical Argument" argues, as discussed earlier, for a "generative ethos" that builds time and opens space, and here we pause to combine both discussions to answer the questions: How does one see the universe of discourse as a palimpsest? How does one "pile time and build space"? How also might one resist the oppressive forces that seek at every turn to end ambiguity by forcing one thing into one meaning? How can we see students, and ourselves, as artists busy at craft?

We propose that kairotic ethos is comprised of the following components:

1. The artistic and destabilizing ability to see texts, people, and places as palimpsests, as continually redrawn figures overlapping earlier figures, faintly seen;
2. A willingness to pause when confronted with a rhetoric of obfuscation;
3. The capacity to recognize and value ambiguities within, between, and among palimpsests without resolving them;
4. The patience to wait until "the right moment to speak or write";
5. The capability to practice *ingenium*, of forging new connections, by living in the interstitial world created by 1–4.

This final component seems most promising for students and teachers of writing, for it suggests kairotic ethos can break through the two-dimensional world of the page and into a third dimension of meaning, the one hiding in between the lines we read and write every day. We read from left to right, and when we reach the margin automatically skip down a line and start again. Perhaps this reading training has bled into training our minds—perhaps because there is no verbal disconnection when we skip down, we assume nothing exists in the spaces we do not occupy.

This essay argues that spaces apparently empty are not bare; neither is language apparently coded gibberish. How might our valuation of the words on the page change if the *boustrophedon* writing practice of the Greeks—writing first left to right, then right to left—had come to dominate English? The term combines the word for oxen (*bous*) and the word for turn (*strephein*): when plowing a field, when one reaches the end of a row, one doesn't pick up the plough and lead the oxen all the way across to the start of a new row. Instead, one simply changes direction. Left to right, right to left, in a long "S" of language tied together.

A kairotic ethos asks us to imagine what we have never imagined, to see the many in the one, to wait in the presence of temptation, to stir uncomfortably without answers, to allow the golden moment, and to weave our own connections from the fractured and fracturing practices that have led us stubbornly from left to right, from dawn to dusk, from the cradle to the grave.

NOTES

1. As the Archimedes Palimpsest website notes, "calling it the Archimedes Palimpsest is a little confusing": on the surface, it is a medieval prayer book, but within the 174 parchment folios are seven treatises by Archimedes ("the Equilibrium of Planes, Spiral Lines, The Measurement of the Circle, Sphere and Cylinder, On Floating Bodies, The Method of Mechanical Theorems, and the Stomachion"). Yet another six pages contains work by the fourth-century Attic orator Hyperides, and some six folios represent the work of an unidentified "Neoplatonic philosophical text." Additionally, four more folios came from "a liturgical book." Last, "twelve further pages come from two different books" ("The Making"). Appropriate to our theme, the more we look at this palimpsest, the more it continues to inform us.

2. The following sources come from the Liddell and Scott entry on "Amphibolos" accessed through the Perseus Project.

3. Liddell and Scott cite Euripides's *Ion*, where Cruesa reveals to her son Ion that his true father is Apollo. She neither fed nor washed the child; the only thing she did for baby Ion was to fit him with swaddling clothes. The Greek: "*parthenia d' emas materos / spargan' amphibola soi tad' enêpsa, ker- / kidos emas planous.*" In English: "I fitted around you these baby-clothes, the work of my flying shuttle." In Liddell and Scott's second example, *amphobolos* occurs in Euripides's *The Trojan Women*, where it refers to the net used to haul "an Argive band" sacrifice to Pallas: "and with nooses of cord they dragged it, as it had been a ship's dark hull." The Greek text "*klôstou d' amphibolois linoio naos hôsei*" might also be rendered "encompassing with a flaxen web like a ship [they dragged]." In *Ion*, *amphibola* means something very close to "clothed"; in *Trojan Women* it describes the mechanical means whereby the captive Trojans were moved. Indisputably, both contexts are harrowing (a new mother purposefully abandoning her newborn, and a tricked group of captives about to be slaughtered), but the nature of the word is literal—baby Ion was encompassed by swaddling clothes; the Argives were encompassed by a net.

4. Here Liddell and Scott cite Plato's *Cratylas* 437a "Let us first take up again the word 'episteme' and see how *ambiguous* it is"; Xenophon's *Memorobilia* 35, "'Well then,' said Socrates, 'that there may be *no question* raised about my obedience [. . .]'"; and Thucydides's *The Peloponnesian War 4.18.4* "*tagatha es amphibolon asphalôs ethento*": "prudently accounted their good fortune as *doubtful.*" This second and dominant meaning (ambiguity with a negative connotation), with few exceptions, exists in opposition to the law of noncontradiction. It's doubtful mere happenstance explains why Plato—in his first warning after stating the law—summons that claustrophobic ensnarement, that beset-on-all-sides feeling of *amphobolos.* Though ostensibly the *Cratylas* examines the question of whether language is composed of signs whose meanings are intrinsic or whose meanings are arbitrary, Charles H. Kahn maintains that "the study of words is not and cannot be of any use at all in discovering the nature of things." Moreover, "the study of names suggests that all things are in motion or in flux [. . .] in fact there must be fixed and immutable objects (namely, the Forms) if knowledge and discourse are to be possible at all" (153). Thus, for Plato in this dialogue, the word for knowledge seems both in motion and in flux, an ambiguity that, like the broader question of the nature of linguistic signs, must be resolved: no, a man whose hands are in motion but whose body is at rest cannot said to be both in motion and at rest.

Xenophon's apologia takes up some of the charges not addressed in Plato's *Apologia*; the short quotation here addresses the charge that he led the youth to despise democracy. "Socrates" uses the negative *mê amphibolon êi* to indicate the opposite of ambiguous: in order for there to be no question about his obedience to law, he asks Charicles to fix the specific age of "the young." Considering the trial of Socrates, the multiple ironies of Socrates's professing "obedience to law" through the negation of ambiguity offers up much material for thought.

5. In a third example (there are over a dozen in this list), the historian Thucydides uses *amphilibolon* in a somewhat positive usage that harkens back to Greek mythology and the understanding that Fortune is fickle. While good, it is welcome; when it turns, as it inevitably will, the previously happy cry outrage. This understanding offers up a rare instance of the benefits of ambiguity in the classical imagination—unsettled things, good fortune, and luck are to be enjoyed against their probable loss. Perhaps the best articulation of the nature of Fortune can be found in Boethius's *Consolation of Philosophy*. The character of Philosophy comes to console the condemned Boethius, who has lately come to feel betrayed by Fortune, who had previously smiled upon him: "Change is [Fortune's] normal behavior, her true nature. [. . .]You have discovered the changing face of the random goddess" (23). Because Fortune's nature is itself fickle, no luck must hold out for long, and in a phrase completely in keeping with the discussion from Thucydides, Boethius writes, "all luck is good luck to the man who bears it with equanimity" (31).

6. Interestingly, the way modern readers encounter the notebooks is through a modern type of palimpsest: the various notebooks that act as the source material have been brought together and reordered as if they were a completed text.

7. Given the dominance of word processors, the modern-day analogy to this method would be to simply turn off one's screen while typing.

8. "The ultimate triumph is for an author to become perfectly clear, like glass or air—forgotten by a reader until the story is finished. James Boswell is transparent; Samuel Johnson's life shines through. John McPhee vanishes; geology, oranges, and nuclear physics seem obvious. William Shakespeare disappears; a stage becomes the world, mere players turn into real people, and lines from a script are now familiar in our mouths as household words. Pellucidity. . . ." ("Invisible Writing").

9. Blau goes on to build a conceptual framework for his invisible writing experiment, using James Moffett's process of decentering, where writers move outward in perspective, that is, from the more experiential (describing, narrating) toward the more abstract (analyzing, arguing, theorizing). Moffett's process framework provides writers with a wider perspective on the same phenomena or topic. Like so much of the work on process theory during this period, taxonomies of discourse were used to illustrate the recursiveness of invention. It certainly is true many teachers seized on some of this work to build a slightly different curriculum but still modes-based, as Max-

ine Hairston discusses in "Winds of Change." Blau, however, shows through sequenced writing assignments how this framework can be used as an invention strategy for writers to gain greater fluency as they gave increasingly thoughtful attention to one topic or task. Again, he draws on invisible writing; his participants were twenty-five teachers enrolled in the South Coast Writing Project at the University of California, Santa Barbara. His invisible writing experiment this time was based on Moffett's kinds of discourse. Each student took five to ten minutes on writing tasks of increasing complexity: (1) what is happening (e.g., a journal entry focusing on some emotion evoked by something going on now, probably descriptive writing), (2) what happened, or will happen (e.g., a kind of memoir writing focusing on narration), (3) what happens, or should happen, selecting one of the topics you've written on in (1) or (2) (e.g., exposition ranging from giving advice to someone who is getting married or divorced, or who is becoming a teacher or a parent)—or write on another topic like the dangers of day-dreaming or the wisdom of reflecting on the past or the problems of student writers. Task 4 is to write a poem in seven minutes. The results of this more structured experiment were the same as the earlier one. The teachers found invisible writing satisfying and valuable; the sequencing encouraged them to give increasingly more thoughtful attention to the topic they had chosen. Even those who didn't stick to a single subject said they wrote with greater fluency and control as they moved through the abstractive ladder. Blau writes that "[m]any found [invisible writing] to be a particularly powerful aid to their concentration and a spur to their creativity.

10. Invisible writing frees the writer from attending to anything except his or her thought.

> The invisibly composing writer cannot look back on a trail of words to mark the progress of his thinking as he writes. He must hold the already articulated portions of his thought in his mind as he continues to develop each separate thought and the flow of connected thoughts that constitute his discourse. This extra burden on the writer's memory is likely to improve the quality of his thinking by keeping him attentive to his thoughts at a level that may be deeper than the surface structure of the words he would otherwise be able to read on the page. It may be that, unable to depend on his own written sentences as cues to his thinking, the invisibly composing writer can tap something closer to the well-springs of his thought— his "inner-speech" or even what Sondra Perl ["Writer-Based Prose"] has called a "felt sense" of meaning. (Blau 306)

Blau conjectures that "invisible writing may help writers to think more deeply and purely on their composing because their words are less likely to get in the way of their thinking" (306).

11. With the social/cultural/political swing in the late 1980s, we seemed to throw out almost wholesale anything pre-postmodernism. Perhaps we might reclaim some of the important work of the 1970s and 1980s. Might we now go beyond postprocess and postmodernism?

WORKS CITED

Aaron, P. G., and Robert G. Clouse. "Freud's Psychohistory of Leonardo da Vinci: A Matter of Being Right or Left." *Journal of Interdisciplinary History* 13.1 (1982): 1–16. Print.

"Amphibolos." *The Perseus Project*. Web. 4 May 2007.

Atwill, Janet M., and Janice M. Lauer, eds. *Perspectives on Rhetorical Invention*. Knoxville: U of Tennessee P, 2002. Print.

Blau, Sheridan. "Invisible Writing: Investigating Cognitive Processes in Composition." *College Composition and Communication* 34.3 (1983): 297–312. Print.

Boethius. *The Consolation of Philosophy*. Trans Victor Watts. London: Penguin, 1999. Print.

Britton, James, et al. *The Development of Writing Abilities, (11–18)*. London: Macmillan Education, 1975. Print.

Brown, Dan. *The Da Vinci Code*. New York: Doubleday, 2003. Print.

Burke, Kenneth. *Language as Symbolic Action*. Berkeley: U of California P, 1978. Print.

Butler, Paul. "Style in the Diaspora of Composition Studies." *Rhetoric Review* 26.1 (2007): 5–24. Print.

Chamberlin, John. *Medieval Arts Doctrines on Ambiguity and Their Places in Langland's Poetics*. Montreal: McGill-Queens UP, 2000. Print.

Corder, Jim. "Argument as Emergence: Rhetoric as Love." *Rhetoric Review* 4 (1985): 16–32. Print.

—. "Varieties of Ethical Argument with Some Account of the Significance of *Ethos* in the Teaching of Composition." *Freshman English News* 6 (1978): 1–23. Print.

Crowley, Sharon, and Debra Hawhee. *Ancient Rhetorics for Contemporary Students*. 4th ed. New York: Longman, 2008.

Dearborn, Jay Edwards. *A Creole Lexicon: Architecture, Landscape, People*. Baton Rouge: Louisiana State UP, 2004. Print.

Delio, Michelle. "Da Vinci: The Pith Behind the Man." Web. 24 Jul 2007.

De Quincey, Thomas. "The Palimpsest of the Human Brain." *Suspira de Profundis*. Edinburgh: Adam and Charles Black, 1871. 10–22. Print.

Enos, Theresa. "Writing, A Driving Force." *Writers on Writing*. Vol. II. Ed. Tom Waldrep. New York: Random, 1988. 67–72. Print.

Friedman, Thomas L. "The Whole World Is Watching." *The New York Times* 27 June 2007: A23. Print.

Hairston, Maxine. "The Winds of Change: Thomas Kuhn and the Revolution in the Teaching of Writing." *College Composition and Communication* 23 (1982): 76–88. Print.

Henry, Walter. "Why Palimpsest?" Web. 24 Jul 2007.

"Invisible Writing." *ZhurnalWiki*. Web. 17 Oct 2007.

Kahn, Charles H. "Language and Ontology in the Cratylus." *Exegesis and Argument: Studies in Greek philosophy presented to Gregory Vlastos.* Ed. Edward N. Lee, Alexander Mourelatos, and Richard Rorty. Assen: Van Gorcum, 1973. 152–76. Print.

Lempriere, John. *Classical Dictionary.* London: Bracken, 1994. Print.

"The Making of a Palimpsest." *The Archimedes Palimpsest.* Web. 31 July 2007.

Moffett, James. *Teaching the Universe of Discourse.* Boston, MA: Houghton Mifflin, 1968. Print.

Orwell, George. *1984.* New York: Penguin Group, 1977. Print.

"The Palimpsest." *The Archimedes Palimpsest.* Web. 25 Jul 2007.

"Palimpsest, *n.* and *adj.*" *The Oxford English Dictionary Online.* Web. 1 Aug 2007.

Perl, Sondra. "Understanding Composing." *College Composition and Communication* 31 (1980): 363–69. Print.

—. "Writer-Based Prose: A Cognitive Basis for Problems in Writing." *College English* 41 (1979): 19–37. Print.

Plato. *The Republic.* Trans. A. D. Lindsay. New York: Knopf, 1992. Print.

—. *The Republic in Two Volumes.* Trans. Paul Shorey. Cambridge, MA: Harvard UP, 1946. Print

"The Republic, IV." *The Internet Classics Archive.* Trans. Benjamin Jowett. Web. 6 May 2007.

Richter, Jean Paul. *The Notebooks of Leonardo Da Vinci Compiled and Edited from the Original Manuscripts By Jean Paul Richter.* New York: Dover, 1970. Print.

Roughton, Becke. "Power of the Blank Page." *College Composition and Communication* 28.3 (1977): 239. Print.

Seidman, Dov. *How.* New York: Wiley, 2007. Print.

Zwijnenberg, Robert. *The Writings and Drawings of Leonardo da Vinci: Order and Chaos in Early Modern Thought.* Trans. Caroline A. van Eck. Cambridge: Cambridge UP, 1999. Print.

Index

Contributors

Thomas Black is a PhD student at the University of Nevada, Reno where he teaches and conducts research in digital rhetoric with focus on Burkean theories in a digital environment. He is also active in core writing assessment, computers in the classroom, and writing across the curriculum programs. He has participated in several rhetoric and composition conferences including the Rhetoric Society of America, Feminisms and Rhetorics, and several others.

Shane Borrowman is a freelance writer and Assistant Professor of English at The University of Montana Western. He is a frequent contributor to *Renaissance Magazine*, writing on topics as diverse as medieval Islamic studies, the astrolabe, and the *Malleus Maleficarium*. His recent publications include the co-edited collection *Rhetoric in the Rest of the West* and the textbook *The Cost of Business*. He enjoys zombie movies and finds it harder each year to root for the New England Patriots.

Crystal Broch-Colombini is a doctoral candidate in rhetoric and composition at the University of Nevada, Reno. Her interest in the field developed from several years spent teaching composition at the Southwest University of Science and Technology in Mianyang, China. Her current research interests include the rhetoric of public and media discourses, feminist rhetoric, and writing program administration. She has presented at numerous conferences, including WPA, Thomas R. Watson, and Feminisms and Rhetorics.

Richard Leo Enos is Professor and Holder of the Lillian Radford Chair of Rhetoric and Composition at Texas Christian University. His research concentration is in classical rhetoric with an emphasis in the relationship between oral and written discourse. He is the Past President of the Rhetoric Society of America and former Editor of *Advances in the History of Rhetoric*. In 2006 he was awarded the George E. Yoos Distinguished

Service Award by the Rhetoric Society of America and was inducted as an RSA Fellow.

Theresa Enos is Professor of English at The University of Arizona. Founder and editor of *Rhetoric Review*, she teaches both graduate and undergraduate courses in writing and rhetoric. Her research interests include the history and theory of rhetoric and the intellectual work and politics of rhetoric and composition studies. She has edited or coedited eleven books, including the *Encyclopedia of Rhetoric and Composition, The Writing Program Administrator's Resource: A Guide to Reflective Institutional Practice,* and *The Promise and Perils of Writing Program Administration,* and she has published numerous chapters and articles on rhetorical theory and issues in writing. She is the author of *Gender Roles and Faculty Lives in Rhetoric and Composition* (1996), and she served as president of the Council of Writing Program Administrators (1997–99) and as Director of the Rhetoric, Composition, and the Teaching of English graduate program at The University of Arizona (1997–2004).

Daniel R. Fredrick is Assistant Professor of Writing Studies at the American University of Sharjah. He earned his PhD in rhetoric and composition from Texas Christian University. In addition to studying classical rhetoric, the ancient world, and EFL writing pedagogy, he often travels to places important to the history of rhetoric, particularly Rome (to pay homage).

Shawn Fullmer is an Associate Professor of English at Fort Lewis College in Durango Colorado, where he teaches persuasive writing, writing pedagogy, and rhetorical theory. He is the co-author of "Emerging (Web)Sites for Writing Centers" and has presented at numerous national conferences on the topic of writing technologies.

Joseph Jones is an Assistant Professor in the Professional Writing and Composition Studies concentration at the University of Memphis, where he has also directed the First-Year Composition program. His research interests include publications exploring histories of rhetoric and composition, composition pedagogy, writing assessment, and the intersections and estrangements of college and secondary school English.

Marcia Kmetz is a PhD candidate in rhetoric and composition at the University of Nevada, Reno, where she studies rural identity, civic discourse, and the rustic in ancient rhetoric. She has presented her work at a variety of conferences including CCCC, WPA, Feminisms and Rhetorics,

Thomas R. Watson, Western States Rhetoric and Literacy Conference, and the Rhetoric Society of America. Current research projects include an inquiry into the anti-war rhetoric of Jeannette Rankin between her terms in Congress, an investigation into the rustic figure in ancient Greek and Roman rhetoric, and a review of the rhetoric of deficiency surrounding the issue of autism.

Rob Lively is a tenured faculty member at Truckee Meadows Community College, as well as a PhD student in rhetoric and composition at the University of Nevada, Reno. His research interests include the connections between rhetoric and creative writing, writing program administration, and science fiction in popular culture. He has presented at the WPA conference, the Midwest PCA, and the national Popular Culture Association conference. He has published essays in *The X-Files and Literature* and *Future Visions: Key Science Fiction and Fantasy Television Texts*.

Richard William Rawnsley received his MA in rhetoric and composition from California State University, San Bernardino and is currently Associate Professor of English at College of the Desert in Palm Desert, California. His work focuses on English composition. Before returning to school to earn bachelor's and master's degrees, he worked for many years as a printer and typographer in print shops, advertising agencies, magazines, and newspapers. During that time he made a personal study of the "art preservative of all arts."

Sherry Rankins-Robertson holds a dual lectureship in Humanities and Arts and Multimedia Writing and Technical Communication at Arizona State University-Polytechnic. In addition to publishing *The Instructor's Manual for Kolin's Successful Writing at Work*, 8th ed., Sherry has co-written instructional materials on writing strategies in the basic writing classroom and peer review with Duane Roen. Sherry completed her Master of Arts in Professional and Technical Writing at University of Arkansas-Little Rock. To complete her doctorate in the Rhetoric/Composition/Linguistics program at Arizona State University, Sherry's dissertation work examines family research and writing in the first-year composition classroom.

Duane Roen is Professor of English at Arizona State University, where he serves as Head of Humanities and Arts in the School of Applied Arts and Sciences. At Arizona State University he served as Director of Composition for four years before directing ASU's Center for Learning and Teaching Excellence. Prior to that, he directed the Writing Program at Syracuse University, as well as the graduate program in Rhetoric, Composition, and the Teaching of English at The University of Arizona. In addition to more than 160 articles, chapters, and conference papers, Duane has published the following books: *Composing Our Lives in Rhetoric and Composition: Stories About the Growth of a Discipline* (with Theresa Enos and Stuart Brown); *The Writer's Toolbox* (with Stuart Brown and Bob Mittan); *A Sense of Audience in Written Discourse* (with Gesa Kirsch); *Becoming Expert: Writing and Learning Across the Disciplines* (with Stuart Brown and Bob Mittan); *Richness in Writing: Empowering ESL Students* (with the late Donna Johnson); *Strategies for Teaching First-Year Composition* (with Lauren Yena, Susan K. Miller, Veronica Pantoja, and Eric Waggoner); *Views from the Center: The CCCC Chairs' Addresses, 1977–2005*; and *The McGraw-Hill Guide: Writing for College, Writing for Life* (with Greg Glau and Barry Maid).

Jason Thompson is a PhD candidate at The University of Arizona, currently finishing his dissertation entitled *'A Kind of Thing that Might Be': Toward a Poetics of New Media*. His research interests include new media, Kenneth Burke, classical rhetoric, and poetics.

Kathleen Blake Yancey is Kellogg W. Hunt Professor of English at Florida State University, where she also directs the graduate program in Rhetoric and Composition Studies. Past President of the Council of Writing Program Administrators and Past Chair of the Conference on College Composition and Communication, she is President of the National Council of Teachers of English. She also co-directs the International Coalition on Electronic Portfolio Research, which has brought together over forty-five institutions to focus on and document the learning that takes place inside and around electronic portfolios. She is the author, editor, or coeditor of ten books and over sixty chapters and refereed articles. Her edited, coedited, and single-authored books include *Portfolios in the Writing Classroom* (1992), *Assessing Writing across the Curriculum* (1997), *Electronic Portfolios* (2001), *Teaching Literature as Reflective Practice* (2004), and *Delivering College Composition; The Fifth Canon* (2006). Her current projects include the volume based on her CCCC Chair's Address, *Composition in a New Key: A Theory and Practice of Composition in the 21st Century*.